THE ARABIC-ENGLISH TRANSLATOR AS PHOTOGRAPHER

It is a useful book with clear definitions, practical examples, and insightful summary questions. It will be most welcome for those willing to ground their intuitions on translation on more solid linguistic foundations.

Qing Cao, Durham University, UK

A masterful book that offers a rich, profound and distinctive study on translation. Invaluable and very practical for students, instructors and researchers who regularly deal with the translation of various kinds of texts between Arabic and English. Through relating linguistics to translation, the authors are shedding light on the multidimensional and interdisciplinary aspect of translation and on the fundamental dynamics that underlie the constant evolution of translation studies.

Andree Affeich, Lebanese American University, Lebanon

The approach employed in *The Arabic-English Translator as Photographer* is novel and the application of the adopted theoretical concepts to explain the process of translation, as opposed to the traditional text-linguistic, discourse analysis or stylistic concepts, is challenging. The examples and explanations are quite appropriate and make life easier for the reader, be they learners, instructors or translators.

Raymond Chakhachiro, Western Sydney University, Australia

The Arabic-English Translator as Photographer is ground breaking and presents innovation in the field of translation as it introduces a detailed description of the processes involved in creating the mental image translators conjure in their minds in the process of translating. . . . The book serves as a thorough yet accessible introduction to structural and interpretive semiotics, functional and cognitive grammar, semantics and cognitive linguistics. Hence, it is great resource for both students and researchers new to the field and scholars from neighbouring disciplines.

Ruba Khamam, University of Leeds, UK

By choosing to use different linguistic approaches as a theoretical basis of their study of translation as a process of picture-taking, *The Arabic-English Translator as Photographer: A Linguistic Account* offers readers an original view of the translator's work.

In addition to laying emphasis on the importance of giving full consideration to the mental image(s) conjured up in the mind of the translators, the book provides an accessible introduction to structural semiotics, interpretive semiotics, functional grammar, semantics and cognitive linguistics for students and researchers who are new to the field. The book can be used as a basis for (post)graduate students, especially students of MA and PhD in Translation Studies as well as students in modern languages schools.

The book focuses on a specific pair of languages, English and Arabic, and presents the relationships generated by texts' translation, including adverts and other types of texts, between these two languages.

Ali Almanna has a PhD in Translation Studies from Durham University (UK) and MA in Linguistics and Translation from Westminster University (UK). Currently, he is teaching Linguistics and Translation in the department of English, Al-Zahra College for Women. His recent publications include *'The Routledge Course in Translation Annotation'*, *'Semantics for Translation Students'* and *'The Nuts and Bolts of Arabic-English Translation'*.

Khaled Al-Shehari is Assistant Professor at Sultan Qaboos University, Oman. He holds an MSc (1998) and a PhD (2001) in Translation Studies from the University of Manchester, UK. He has published articles in *The Interpreter* and *Translator Trainer*, *Translation Studies in the New Millennium*, and edited collections.

THE ARABIC-ENGLISH TRANSLATOR AS PHOTOGRAPHER

A Linguistic Account

Ali Almanna and Khaled Al-Shehari

LONDON AND NEW YORK

First published 2019
by Routledge
2 Park Square, Milton Park, Abingdon, Oxon OX14 4RN

and by Routledge
52 Vanderbilt Avenue, New York, NY 10017

Routledge is an imprint of the Taylor & Francis Group, an informa business

© 2019 Ali Almanna and Khaled Al-Shehari

The right of Ali Almanna and Khaled Al-Shehari to be identified as authors of this work has been asserted by them in accordance with sections 77 and 78 of the Copyright, Designs and Patents Act 1988.

All rights reserved. No part of this book may be reprinted or reproduced or utilized in any form or by any electronic, mechanical, or other means, now known or hereafter invented, including photocopying and recording, or in any information storage or retrieval system, without permission in writing from the publishers.

Trademark notice: Product or corporate names may be trademarks or registered trademarks, and are used only for identification and explanation without intent to infringe.

British Library Cataloguing-in-Publication Data
A catalogue record for this book is available from the British Library

Library of Congress Cataloging-in-Publication Data
A catalog record for this book has been requested

ISBN: 978-1-138-06825-4 (hbk)
ISBN: 978-1-138-06828-5 (pbk)
ISBN: 978-1-315-15810-5 (ebk)

Typeset in Bembo
by Apex CoVantage, LLC

CONTENTS

Acknowledgements   vii
Note on transliteration   ix
List of abbreviations and symbols   xi

1   Setting the scene: introductory matters   1

     Who is the book for? 1
     Why is it different? 2
     Structure of the book 3
     Hypotheses and research questions 4
     Significance of the book 5
     Theoretical background 6

2   Signs and syntagmatic and paradigmatic axes   14

     Semiotics 14
     Signified versus signifier 16
     Syntagms and paradigms 18
     Commutation test 26

3   A sign's functions and intertextuality   32

     Peirce's interpretive semiotics 32
        Iconic function 34
        Indexical function 36
        Symbolic function 39
     Intertextuality 47

4 Transitivity system 59

　Transitivity 59
　　Material processes 60
　　Mental processes 62
　　Verbal processes 64
　　Behavioural processes 66
　　Relational processes 68
　　Existential processes 70
　Circumstances 71

5 Semantic roles and flow of energy 82

　Arguments and types of semantic roles 82
　Verb-specific semantic roles 86
　Grammatical relations and semantic roles 90
　Energy transfer and mental contact 98

6 Imaging systems I: the configurational system 106

　Plexity 106
　State of boundedness 109
　State of dividedness 112
　Disposition of a quantity 113
　Degree of extension 114
　Pattern of distribution 115
　Axiality 116
　Scene partitioning 116

7 Imaging systems II: attention, perspective and force dynamics 122

　Distribution of attention 122
　Force dynamics 128
　Deployment of perspective 132
　　Location 132
　　Distance 133
　　Mode 135
　　Direction 136

Index *141*

ACKNOWLEDGEMENTS

Our deep indebtedness and sincere appreciation naturally go to Leonard Talmy of the University at Buffalo (US), who provided us with useful comments and advice.

We owe a debt of gratitude to many people for their meticulous feedback on the manuscript. In particular, we would like to thank: Qing Cao (University of Durham, UK), Murtadha J. Bakir (Philadelphia University, Jordan), Shihab Ahmed Al-Nassir (University of Basrah, Iraq), James Dickins (University of Leeds, UK), Ashraf Abdul-Fattah (Hamad Bin Khalifa University, Qatar), Abdul-Sahib Ali (University of Sharjah, UAE), Hashim Q. Lazim (Shatt Al-Arab University College, Iraq), Orhan Elmaz (University of St Andrews, UK), Jawad Kadhim Jabir (University of Basrah, Iraq), Raymond Chakhachiro (Western Sydney University, Australia), Khaled Shakir (University of Thi Qar, Iraq), Hassan Gadalla (Assiut University, Egypt), Fida Al-Mawla (Wasit University, Iraq), Muhammad Fawzi Alghazi (Alexandria University, Egypt), Ali Talib Jabboori (Tikrit University, Iraq), Juan José Martínez-Sierra (Universitat de València, Spain), Aqeel Al-Hamedi (Shatt Al-Arab University College, Iraq), Nicolas Froeliger (Université Paris Diderot, Paris 7, France), Andree Affeich (Lebanese American University, Lebanon), Mustapha Taibi (Western Sydney University, Australia), Ali Al-Hassnawi (University of Buraimi, Sultanate of Oman), Jasim Al-Maryani (University of Basrah, Iraq), Mohammed Al-Sha'rawi (University of Nizwa, Sultanate of Oman), Ammar Fouad (University of Basrah, Iraq), Nhat Tuan Nguyen (Hanoi University, Vietnam), Khaled Tawfik (Cairo University, Egypt) and Ali Mohammed Hussein (University of Basrah, Iraq).

Our special thanks also go to Fred Pragnell and Ibrahem Ibrahem, who offered valuable insights into, and guidance on, the many and varied aspects of the linguistic and analytical challenges of translating Arabic.

In addition, we would like to thank the BA and MA students of Arabic-English translation over the years at the University of Nizwa (Sultanate of Oman) and the University of Basrah (Iraq), whose translation projects have served as sources for the translation examples used in this book.

Our special thanks also go to Laṯīf as-Samḫān for providing us with permission to use some of his paintings in this book.

Our sincere appreciation naturally goes to Jawad Al-Mudhafer and Doha Al-Saied, who helped us in drawing the paintings used in the book.

Finally, no words could ever express our deepest love and gratitude to our families, who have supported us in this work.

NOTE ON TRANSLITERATION

The following Arabic transliteration system has been consistently employed throughout this book. However, in the case of ˊ *shaddah*, a consonant is doubled. The names of Arab authors whose works have been published in English are spelled as they appear in the publication without applying this transliteration system. In addition, any Arab names that appear in quotations follow the transliteration system of the reference quoted and not that listed below. Some names, such as Mahfouz, Choukri and the like, remain as they commonly appear in English and have not been transliterated in order to avoid confusion.

Arabic	*Transliteration*	*Arabic*	*Transliteration*
ء	ʾ	ط	ṭ
ب	b	ظ	ẓ
ت	t	ع	ʿ
ث	th	غ	gh
ج	j	ف	f
ح	ḥ	ق	q
خ	kh	ك	k
د	d	ل	l
ذ	dh	م	m
ر	r	ن	n
ز	z	ة/هـ	h
س	s	و	w
ش	sh	ي	y
ص	ṣ	ا/ى	a
ض	ḍ		

Vowels

fat_h_ah	a
kasrah	i
_d_ammah	u
alif	ā
yaa'	ī
waaw	ū

ABBREVIATIONS AND SYMBOLS

Abbreviations

Adj	adjective
Adv	adverb
Det	determiner
Infl	inflection
NP	noun phrase
P	preposition
PP	prepositional phrase
S	sentence
SL	source language
ST	source text
Sth	something
TL	target language
TT	target text
V	verb
VP	verb phrase

Symbols

Ø	nothing
^^	indicates there is an addition, omission or manipulation through translation
=	indicates there is no addition, omission or manipulation through translation
#	indicates a suggested translation or an example written for the purposes of this course

1
SETTING THE SCENE
Introductory matters

The market does not need yet another book on translation theory, practice or didactics as it is crammed full of titles that range from translation between *A* and *B*, translation between theory and practice, thinking translation, introduction to translation, principles of translation and the like to titles that focus on the text type, such as legal translation, literary translation, business translation and so on.

The Arabic-English Translator as Photographer, like other books on the market, tries to cover certain aspects of translation as a product (i.e. translation) and translation as a process (i.e. translating) by consolidating theoretical claims taken from neighbouring disciplines (e.g. semiotics, semantics, functional grammar, visual grammar and cognitive linguistics) with authentic translational data. Theoretical issues are presented in this book in a friendly, clear and comprehensive way, supported with ample authentic examples taken from different sources.

Who is the book for?

The Arabic-English Translator as Photographer is an academic textbook that can be used as a basis for (post)graduate students, especially students of MA and PhD in Translation Studies, as well as undergraduate students in modern language schools all over the world. The intended audience for our book is:

1 Postgraduate and advanced BA students along with their translation teachers throughout the world,
2 MA and PhD students in translation, intercultural studies and contrastive studies, and
3 Students of linguistics in general, and semiotics, semantics, functional grammar, visual grammar and cognitive linguistics in particular.

Why is it different?

In addition to laying an emphasis on the importance of considering the mental image(s) conjured up in the minds of the translators, the book provides an accessible introduction to structural semiotics, interpretive semiotics, functional grammar, semantics and cognitive linguistics for students and researchers who are new to the field. The book can also serve as a work of reference for translators (be they students or professionals), translation researchers and translation instructors on the one hand and, on the other hand, for researchers and scholars from neighbouring disciplines.

Our aim is to provide the reader with an engaging and accessible academic book. Therefore, whenever necessary, we provide them with some details, including the definitions of some terms and relevant citations in the running text in order to provide the readers with a route into the primary literature needed. Among the significant concepts introduced in this book are *semiotics, sign, signified, signifier, paradigmatic axis* and *syntagmatic axis, iconic function, indexical function, symbolic function, intertextuality, transitivity system, semantic roles, energy transfer, narrative, plexity, state of dividedness, state of boundedness, degree of extension, pattern of distribution, axiality, scene partitioning, foregrounding, backgrounding, windowing of attention, scope of attention, profile selection, scope of intention, extent of causation, force dynamics* and finally the *perspectival system* along with its four schematic categories, i.e. *location, distance, mode* and *direction*.

There are a number of books on the market that explain semiotics, semantics, functional grammar, visual grammar and cognitive linguistics. Following are just a few examples:

Carter, R. (1998). *Vocabulary: Applied Linguistic Perspectives*. London/New York: Routledge.

Evans, V. and Green, M. (2006). *Cognitive Linguistics: An Introduction*. Edinburgh: Edinburgh University Press.

Goodman, S. (1996). "Visual English". In S. Goodman and D. Graddol (eds.), *Redesigning English: New Text, New Identities*. London/New York: Routledge.

Halliday, M. A. K. (1994). *An Introduction to Functional Grammar* (2nd edn). London et al.: Arnold.

Johnson, M. (1987). *The Body in the Mind: The Bodily Basis of Meaning, Imagination, and Reason*. Chicago: University of Chicago Press.

Langacker, R. ([1991] 2002). *Concept, Image, Symbol: The Cognitive Basis of Grammar* (2nd edn). Berlin: Mouton de Gruyter.

Lee, D. (2001). *Cognitive Linguistics: An Introduction*. Oxford: Oxford University Press.

Lyons, J. (1977). *Semantics*. Cambridge: Cambridge University Press.

Pertilli, S. (1992). "Translation, Semiotics and Ideology", *TTR: Traduction, Terminologie, Rédaction*, Vol. 5 (1), pp. 233–264.

Riemer, N. (2010). *Introducing Semantics*. Cambridge: Cambridge University Press.

Saeed, J. I. (2009). *Semantics* (3rd edn). Oxford/West Sussex: Wiley Blackwell.

Talmy, L. (2000). *Toward a Cognitive Semantics: Vol. 1: Concept Structuring Systems*. Cambridge: MIT Press.

Taylor, J. (2002). *Cognitive Grammar*. Oxford: Oxford University Press.

Ungerer, H. and Friedrich, S. (1996). *An Introduction to Cognitive Linguistics*. London: Longman.

However, none of these books have approached the topic from a translation or contrastive point of view. Further, none of them have taken the language pair of Arabic-English as its focus.

On the other hand, despite the great number of translation programmes (at both the undergraduate and postgraduate levels) worldwide, a small number of academic publications take the language pair (Arabic-English) as their focus. Here are some:

Almanna, A. (2016a). *The Routledge Course in Translation Annotation: Arabic-English-Arabic*. London/New York: Routledge.

———. (2016b). *Semantics for Translation Students: Arabic-English-Arabic*. Oxford: Peter Lang.

Dickins, J. et al. (2002). *Thinking Arabic Translation*. London/New York: Routledge.

El-Farahaty, H. (2014). *Arabic-English-Arabic Legal Translation*. London/New York: Routledge.

Farghal, M. and Almanna, A. (2015). *Contextualizing Translation Theories: Aspects of Arabic – English Interlingual Communication*. Newcastle upon Tyne, England: Cambridge Scholars Publishing.

Hatim, B. (1997). *English-Arabic/Arabic-English Translation: A Practical Guide*. London: Saqi Books.

Husni, R. and Newman, D. (2015). *Arabic-English-Arabic Translation*. London/New York: Routledge.

Unlike some of the publications mentioned above, which confine themselves to a particular text type or a perspective, this book explores both directions (i.e. out of Arabic and into Arabic). Further, it focuses on the mental images conjured up in the mind of the translator while translating a text from language *A* to language *B*. These images are studied from different perspectives in this book.

The book features original materials taken from a wide range of sources, including literary texts, journalistic texts, religious texts, technical texts and advertisements.

Structure of the book

This book has seven chapters which can be sketched as follows:

Chapter 1 tries to justify why an interpretive approach is used as a framework for describing the process of translation at its micro level. Further, an attempt is made to explain how translating can be seen as a process of picture-taking. To this end, the work of translators is compared to that of photographers who, for a variety of different reasons, intervene to adjust the image resolution, thus producing a picture that may satisfy the client but misleads others or the other way around.

In Chapter 2, issues such as signs, signifieds, signifiers, and paradigmatic and syntagmatic axes are discussed in a direct link to the actual work of the translator.

4 Setting the scene

Further, in this chapter, syntagmatic and paradigmatic axes are used as parameters to test the significance of the sign and, accordingly, the translation accuracy.

Chapter 3 focuses on the sign's functions (be it iconic, indexical or symbolic) and their importance in the actual act of translating between two languages as culturally distant as Arabic and English. In addition to these three main functions, the intertextual relationships established between the set of signs are viewed through the prism of translation.

In Chapter 4, transitivity processes according to Halliday's systemic functional grammar as to whether they represent an event, action, saying, behaviour, state of mind, state of being or state of existing are presented and discussed with reference to translation.

Chapter 5 gives full consideration to the semantic roles assigned to each noun phrase in the clause. It is held in this chapter that in order to create a similar mental image in our readers' minds, adequate consideration should be given to these semantic roles filled by each argument.

Chapters 6 and 7 are devoted to discussing imaging systems which are classified by Talmy (2000) into four systems, namely (1) the configurational system, (2) the perspectival system, (3) the attentional system and (4) the force-dynamic system. Chapter 6 confines itself to the first system in the imaging systems, that is, the configurational system, which refers to all forms of conceptualization of quantity or relations between quantities in dimensions like TIME and SPACE. Seven schematic categories (i.e. 'plexity', 'state of dividedness', 'state of boundedness', 'degree of extension', 'pattern of distribution', 'axiality' and 'scene partitioning') that form the configurational system are discussed in this chapter in a direct link with translation. Chapter 7, on the other hand, focuses on the other imaging systems, that is, the attentional system, the perspectival system and the force-dynamic system.

Hypotheses and research questions

In this book, it is hypothesized that the process of translation at its micro level (i.e. the focus is placed on the work of the translator) is better understood if it is seen as a process of picture-taking. That is, in addition to giving full consideration to the linguistic elements that are used by language users to conceptualize certain socio-cultural experiences, the translators need to take into account the different images conjured up in their minds while translating the text from language A to language B. This hypothesis is interpretive as it "asks whether something (X) can be usefully interpreted as Y, or better understood if we 'see it' as something else" (Saldanha and O'Brien 2014: 18). In this regard, Chesterman (2008b: 56) states that interpretive hypotheses are "what we use when we try to understand meaningful yet obscure phenomena". It is further hypothesized that in order to create a similar mental image in the mind of the target-language reader, the translator needs to pay extra attention to:

- the syntagmatic and paradigmatic axes,
- the sign's function and whether it is iconic, indexical or symbolic,
- the process (be it material, mental, verbal, behavioural, relational or existential) along with its participants and circumstances used in the clause,

- the semantic role assigned to each argument in the clause,
- the time lapse between the processes utilized in the source text,
- the action-chain schemas and energy transfer,
- the configurational system,
- the distribution of attention in the depicted scene,
- the deployment of perspective in the depicted scene, and
- the force-dynamic patterns employed in the depicted scene.

Building on these hypotheses, the following research questions are formulated to be addressed throughout the book:

1 What will happen to the mental image if the semantic role assigned to a given argument is changed through translation? Will that affect the mental image?
2 What will happen to the mental image if the path or windowing of attention is changed through translation?
3 What will happen to the mental image if the viewer's location or the distance between him/her and the depicted scene is changed?
4 What will happen to the mental image if the force-dynamic patterns employed in the original text are changed through translation?
5 What will happen to the mental image if the pace of events is sped up or slowed down through translation?
6 What will happen to the mental image if the scope of intention becomes greater than the extent of causation or the other way round?
7 What will happen to the mental image if the process is changed, the circumstance becomes a process or the other way round, a process is added or deleted, etc.? This research question leads to:

   a Can transitivity processes according to Halliday's systemic functional grammar – as to whether they represent an event, action, saying, behaviour, state of mind, state of being or state of existing – be used as parameters to test the translation accuracy?
   b Can these processes be used as a theoretical framework to analyse certain socio-cultural experiences encoded linguistically in a text, regardless of the language itself?

8 Finally, is it enough for the translator to pay attention to the syntagmatic and paradigmatic axes to test the significance of the sign and, accordingly, the accuracy of the mental image(s)?

Significance of the book

Focusing on the image(s) conjured up in the translators' minds (be they trainees or professionals) can be used by the student translators to annotate their own translations or comment on others'. It provides them with a rich soil to academically discuss the local strategies adopted by them while translating or adopted by others when they act as reviewers. By doing so, they will develop the ability to defend their own decisions and/or evaluate others'. Further, it can be employed by the critics, revisers and reviewers to evaluate/assess/review the work of a professional translator in a professional setting. Finally, and most importantly, it can be used by the translation instructors for pedagogical purposes either to analyse and evaluate their students' translations or to explain the process of translation.

Theoretical background

In this book, an *interpretive approach* with a slight modification is adopted to study translation as a process of picture-taking. The interpretive approach (or the *theory of sense* as it is known in the literature) is proposed by a group of scholars known as the Paris School to address conference interpreting-related issues (cf. Salama-Carr 1998: 113–114; Lederer 2003: 23–35; Almanna 2014: 49).

Building on the fact that socio-cultural experiences are mapped and conceptualized by languages differently as each language has its own linguistic system, the proponents of this approach (e.g. Danica Seleskovitch 1975/2002 and Marianne Lederer 1981, 1994/2003) argue that "interpreting [...] is not merely reflecting what is expressed by the original writer/speaker by using corresponding words/expressions" in the target text (Almanna 2014: 49). By doing so, this, as they believe, will result in a text that the target readers may or may not understand, depending on the availability of correspondence in the target text (Lavault 1996: 97 cited in Shuttleworth and Cowie 1997: 85; Almanna 2014: 49).

This approach is divided into three interrelated stages. They are:

1 Understanding

In this stage, the interpreter tries to make every possible effort to understand the original text by forming a personal point of view (Ross 1980: 20). In order to understand the text, the interpreter needs to interact with the text at hand (cf. Lederer 2003: 31; Munday 2008: 63; Albir and Alves 2009: 55). To do so, a number of processes, such as a bottom-up process and top-down process, need to be activated and certain cognitive inputs, such as their encyclopaedic knowledge and their socio-cultural experiences, need to be consulted (cf. Albir and Alves 2009: 55). In this regard, Bell (1991: 235; emphasis his) holds:

> Interactive processing combines bottom-up with top-down which permits processing to take place *simultaneously* in both directions with each process 'feeding' the other with information and, eventually, arriving at an agreed conclusion, unless the data is too degenerate to process or too ambiguous, etc.

2 De-verbalization

In this stage, the actual wording is divorced from the linguistic and stylistic norms. Albir and Alves (2009: 55) state that "the existence of an intermediate phase of deverbalization resulting from the phase of understanding and the beginning of the phase of re-expression" plays a fundamental role in the interpretive approach to the translation process. This is because the reformulation or re-expression stage is "achieved through deverbalized meaning and not on the basis of linguistic form".

3 Re-expression (or reformulation)

In this stage, the interpreter starts searching for an idiomatic means of expression in an attempt to translate the *sense* of the original text by adhering to the usage and customs of the target language.

It is worth mentioning that in an attempt to adopt this approach to translation, Jean Delisle (1980/1988) adds a fourth stage, i.e. *verification*. In this fourth stage, the translator checks and evaluates his/her own translation to make sure that s/he has reflected the intended meaning. Salama-Carr (1998: 114; also discussed in Almanna 2014: 50) comments that this stage, i.e. *verification*, can be "described as a process of back-translation which allows the translator to apply a qualitative analysis of selected solutions and equivalents".

In this book, in addition to adopting this approach to talk about the work of both the translator and interpreter, it is proposed that the first two stages, i.e. *understanding* and *de-verbalizing*, can be looked at as one stage. How? When a text is understood, it is automatically transferred into our mind in the form of images – a picture has been taken. Misunderstanding will lead to slightly or completely different mental image(s), depending on the degree of misunderstanding. To put this differently, these two stages cannot be separated from each other: once a text is understood, it is de-verbalized, that is, certain mental images are conjured up in the mind of the text reader/hearer, as modelled here:

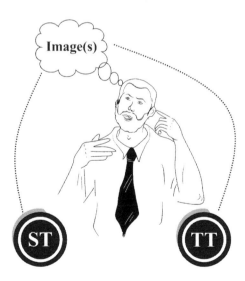

When the reader/hearer fails to understand the text at hand, this means that s/he fails to de-verbalize it, i.e. fails to form mental images. When a group of people read or hear the word *car*, for instance, and they are asked to close their eyes to tell

8 Setting the scene

us about what they see, they will say that they all see a road vehicle, typically with a steering wheel, an engine, four wheels and seats to carry a small number of people.

But when they are asked to tell us about its size, colour, model and the like, they may provide us with different answers. This is because people are different in terms of their background, encyclopaedic knowledge, socio-cultural experiences and so on. With this in mind, we do not expect that the mental images conjured up in the translators' minds are identical, hence their different translations for the same text. This fits hand in glove with W.V. Quine's (1960) *indeterminacy theory*. In his book *Word and Object* (1960), Quine holds that there are not certain criteria on which we evaluate the target text and whether it is good or bad. This justifies why we have more than one translation for the same text. This is because more than one translation can "meet these criteria, and hence that no unique meaning can be assigned to words and sentences" (Almanna 2014: 29; for more details, see Quine 1976, 1992). By way of explanation, the following example taken from a passage given to the level-one students (Dept. of Translation, University of Basrah) to be translated to English on one of their exams (2014) may be considered (for more details on this example, see Chapter 5 of this book):

هدّد اللصُّ الرّجلَ بالسِّكين

As can be observed, by the effect of the preposition ب used before the instrument, i.e. السِّكين *knife*, we have only one meaning in which the knife is with the thief – in our mind's eye we see that the thief holds a knife, as can be shown below:

Setting the scene 9

This sentence has been translated by the majority of the students into TT1. Despite that, other versions can be discussed here (see TT2, TT3 and TT4).

TT1: *The thief threatened the man with the knife.*

Their suggested translation could mean either of the following meanings:

a   The thief used the knife to threaten the man.
b   The thief threatened the man who was holding the knife.

Approached from a cognitive linguistic perspective, the difference between (a) and (b) lies in whether the knife was with the thief (a) or with the man (b). With this in mind, two mental images are conjured up in our mind, as shown below:

TT2: *With the knife, the thief threatened the man.*

By opting for this syntactic structure where the prepositional phrase *with the knife* is fronted, we see in our mind's eye that the knife is with the thief. Therefore, the student translator has managed to reflect this.

TT3: *The man was threatened by the thief with the knife.*

Here, the student translator has opted for the passive form where the Affected Participant, i.e. *the man*, is fronted and the Actor, i.e. *the thief*, preceded by the preposition *by*, is grouped along with the prepositional phrase *with the knife* with the verb phrase. By doing so, the student translator has managed to create a mental image in which the knife is with the thief.

TT4: *The man with the knife was threatened by the thief.*

Here, the prepositional phrase *with the knife* has been grouped by the student translator with the noun phrase *the man*, thus creating a mental image where the knife is with the man.

10 Setting the scene

To finish off this chapter, let us discuss the distance (it is one of many issues that will be discussed in this book) between the presented participants in the following scene encoded in this sentence given to the level-one students (Faculty of Language Studies, Sohar University) to be translated into English for the purposes of this book:

رأى الرجلُ فتاة صغيرة بالناظور.

Without paying attention to the mental image that may be conjured up in their target readers' minds, the majority of the students have opted for *The man saw a little girl with the binoculars*. By virtue of the grammatical form and content specifications adopted by the writer, the readers as viewers are invited to adopt a distal perspective to see the whole distance (indicated by the dotted line) between the two presented participants, as shown here:

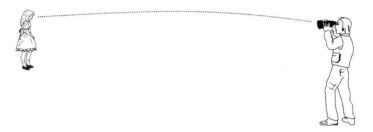

Their suggested translation could mean either of the following meanings:

a   The man saw the girl with the help of the binoculars. This indicates there is a great distance between the presented participants (the man and the girl), hence the use of the binoculars by the man to see the girl, as shown above.
b   The man saw the girl who was holding the binoculars. This indicates that there is no great distance between the presented participants as the man was able to see the girl with the naked eye, as shown below:

As can be noticed, in this mental image, in addition to adding a relational possessive process, that is, *the girl has the binoculars* (see Chapter 4) and changing the semantic role of the noun phrase *the binoculars* from Instrument to Theme (see Chapter 5), the readers as viewers are induced to adopt a proximal perspective as the distance between the man and the girl is not that great (see Chapter 7).

Key technical terms

- De-verbalizing
- Distance
- Indeterminacy theory
- Interpretive approach
- Re-expressing
- Theory of sense
- Verification
- Understanding

Exercises

Exercise 1: In the following four examples, there are three presented participants (*my brother, the girl* and *the hat*) and one presented action (*hit*). However, different syntactic structures are used. Does that affect the mental images conjured up in your mind? In your discussion, try to answer these three questions:

How many mental images? a. _____ b. _____ c. _____ d. _____

Who had the hat? a. _____ b. _____ c. _____ d. _____

Was the hat moved or not? a. _____ b. _____ c. _____ d. _____

a. # *My brother hit the girl with the hat.*
b. # *With the hat, my brother hit the girl.*
c. # *The girl was hit by my brother with the hat.*
d. # *The girl with the hat was hit by my brother.*

Exercise 2: Is there any difference between these two sentences? Do they encode two different scenes or one scene?

The mother of the boy and the girl is leaving the country soon.
The mother of the boy and the girl are leaving the country soon.

Exercise 3: In this chapter, we have discussed when native speakers of English or those who have developed certain linguistic competence in English read or hear the word *car* a mental image is readily conjured up in their minds, regardless of its colour, size, model and the like. Will they have mental images to words such as *happiness, sadness, courage* and *cowardice* without relying on another referent? Discuss.

Further reading

Almanna, A. (2014). *Translation Theories Exemplified from Cicero to Pierre Bourdieu*. München: Lincom Europa Academic Publishers.
Delisle, J. (1980/1988). *L'analyse du discours comme méthode de traduction*. Ottawa, ON: University of Ottawa Press, Part I trans. by P. Logan and M. Creery (1988) as *Translation: An Interpretive Approach*. Ottawa: University of Ottawa Press.
Lederer, M. (1994/2003). *La traduction aujourd'hui: Le modèle interprétatif*. Paris: Hachette, trans. by N. Larché (2003) as *Translation: The Interpretive Model*. Manchester: St Jerome.
Munday, J. (2001/2008). *Introducing Translation Studies: Theories and Applications*. London/New York: Routledge.
Quine, W.V. (1960). *Words and Objects*. Cambridge: MIT Press.
Salama-Carr, M. (1998). "An Interpretive Approach". In M. Baker and K. Malmkjær (eds.), *Routledge Encyclopedia of Translation Studies*. London/New York: Routledge, pp. 112–114.
Seleskovitch, D. (1975/2002). "Language and Memory: A Study of Note-taking in Consecutive Interpreting". In F. Pöchhacker and M. Shlesinger (eds.), *The Interpreting Studies Reader*. London/New York: Routledge, pp. 121–129.

References

Albir, A. H. and Alves, F. (2009). "Translation as a Cognitive Activity". In J. Munday (ed.), *The Routledge Companion to Translation Studies*. London/New York: Routledge.
Almanna, A. (2014). *Translation Theories Exemplified from Cicero to Pierre Bourdieu*. München: Lincom Europa Academic Publishers.
———. (2016a). *The Routledge Course in Translation Annotation: Arabic-English-Arabic*. London/New York: Routledge.
———. (2016b). *Semantics for Translation Students: Arabic-English-Arabic*. Oxford: Peter Lang.
Bell, R.T. (1991). *Translation and Translating: Theory and Practice*. London/New York: Longman.
Carter, R. (1998). *Vocabulary: Applied Linguistic Perspectives*. London/New York: Routledge.
Chesterman, A. (2008b). "The Status of Interpretive Hypotheses". In G. Hansen, A. Chesterman and H. Gerzymisch-Arbogast (eds.), *Efforts and Models in Interpreting and Translation Research*. Amsterdam/Philadelphia: John Benjamins, pp. 49–61.
Delisle, J. (1980/1988). *L'analyse du discours comme méthode de traduction*. Ottawa, ON: University of Ottawa Press, Part I trans. by P. Logan and M. Creery (1988) as *Translation: An Interpretive Approach*. Ottawa: University of Ottawa Press.
Dickins, J. et al. (2002). *Thinking Arabic Translation*. London/New York: Routledge.
El-Farahaty, H. (2014). *Arabic-English-Arabic Legal Translation*. London/New York: Routledge.
Evans, V. and Green, M. (2006). *Cognitive Linguistics: An Introduction*. Edinburgh: Edinburgh University Press.
Farghal, M. and Almanna, A. (2015). *Contextualizing Translation Theories: Aspects of Arabic – English Interlingual Communication*. Newcastle upon Tyne, England: Cambridge Scholars Publishing.
Hatim, B. (1997). *English-Arabic/Arabic-English Translation: A Practical Guide*. London: Saqi Books.
Husni, R. and Newman, D. (2015). *Arabic-English-Arabic Translation*. London/New York: Routledge.
Goodman, S. (1996). "Visual English". In S. Goodman and D. Graddol (eds.), *Redesigning English: New Text, New Identities*. London/New York: Routledge.

Halliday, M. A. K. (1994). *An Introduction to Functional Grammar* (2nd edn). London et al.: Arnold.
Johnson, M. (1987). *The Body in the Mind: The Bodily Basis of Meaning, Imagination, and Reason*. Chicago: University of Chicago Press.
Langacker, R. ([1991] 2002). *Concept, Image, Symbol: The Cognitive Basis of Grammar* (2nd edn). Berlin: Mouton de Gruyter.
Lederer, M. (1981). *La traduction simultanée*. Paris: Minard.
_____. (1994/2003). *La traduction aujourd'hui: Le modèle interprétatif*. Paris: Hachette, trans. by N. Larché (2003) as *Translation: The Interpretive Model*. Manchester: St Jerome.
Lee, D. (2001). *Cognitive Linguistics: An Introduction*. Oxford: Oxford University Press.
Lyons, J. (1977). *Semantics*. Cambridge: Cambridge University Press.
Munday, J. (2001/2008). *Introducing Translation Studies: Theories and Applications*. London/New York: Routledge.
Pertilli, S. (1992). "Translation, Semiotics and Ideology", *TTR: Traduction, Terminologie, Rédaction*, Vol. 5 (1), pp. 233–264.
Quine, W.V. (1960). *Words and Objects*. Cambridge: MIT Press.
_____. (1976). *Ways of Paradox and Other Essays* (Revised in enlarger edition). Cambridge, MA: Harvard University Press.
_____. (1992). *Pursuit of Truth* (2nd edn). Cambridge, MA: Harvard University Press.
Riemer, N. (2010). *Introducing Semantics*. Cambridge: Cambridge University Press.
Ross, S. (ed.) (1980). "Translation and Similarity". In M. Rose (ed.), *Translation Spectrum*, pp. 8–23. Albany: State University of New York Press.
Saeed, J. I. (2009). *Semantics* (3rd edn). Oxford/West Sussex: Wiley Blackwell.
Salama-Carr, M. (1998). "An Interpretive Approach". In M. Baker and K. Malmkjær (eds.), *Routledge Encyclopedia of Translation Studies*, pp. 112–114. London/New York: Routledge.
Saldanha, G. and O'Brien, S. (2014). *Research Methodologies in Translation Studies*. London/New York: Routledge.
Seleskovitch, D. (1975/2002). "Language and Memory: A Study of Note-taking in Consecutive Interpreting". In F. Pöchhacker and M. Shlesinger (eds.), *The Interpreting Studies Reader*, pp. 121–129. London/New York: Routledge.
Shuttleworth, M. and Cowie, M. (1997). *Dictionary of Translation Studies*. Manchester: St. Jerome.
Talmy, L. (2000). *Toward a Cognitive Semantics: Vol. 1: Concept Structuring Systems*. Cambridge: MIT Press.
Taylor, J. (2002). *Cognitive Grammar*. Oxford: Oxford University Press.
Ungerer, H. and Friedrich, S. (1996). *An Introduction to Cognitive Linguistics*. London: Longman.

2
SIGNS AND SYNTAGMATIC AND PARADIGMATIC AXES

In this chapter, signs are given full consideration. A sign, by dictionary definition, is "an object, quality, or event whose presence or occurrence indicates the probable presence or occurrence of something else" (www.oxforddictionaries.com). This means that there are two elements: while the first one is in the real world that can be seen, heard, smelled, realized, etc. the other is evoked by virtue of the first one in the mind of the experiencer/perceiver. This indicates that there should be a relationship between these two elements; otherwise, the object, quality, event, etc. will not invoke in the mind of the user any sign. To study "how people make sense of their experience of the world and how cultures share and give currency to this understanding", one needs to adopt a semiotic approach (Grutman 2009: 261). In what follows, semiotics as the study of signs is briefly discussed before we move on to study the signs through the prism of translation.

Semiotics

The most common definition of 'semiotics' is that it is the study of signs, but Stam et al. (1992: 1) give a wider definition of semiotics as "the study of signs, signification and signifying systems". Approached from such a perspective, Faiq and Sabry (2013: 47) comment that semiotics is "the study of the methods in which local populations communicate through signs and symbols that are obviously influenced by cultural traditions". Moreover, semioticians are also interested in studying how meanings are constructed through certain sets of socio-cultural norms. Thus Fiske and Hartley suggest that the relationship between a sign and its meaning and the way signs are structured into codes are the main concerns of semiotics (1978: 37).

Charles Morris (1972: 15 cited in Nöth 1990: 50; also discussed in Al-Shehari 2001: 104; Almanna 2016b: 162) divides the subject of semiotics into three branches:

- *Semantic*, where the concern is the meaning of signs and their relationship to what they stand for,
- *Syntactic*, which deals with the structural relations between signs, and
- *Pragmatic*, the study of the ways in which signs are used and interpreted.

Fiske (1990:40) outlines three main areas of study covered by semiotics. First, there is the study of the *sign* itself, which relates to the investigation of different varieties of signs that represent meanings in different ways, and the ways in which people understand and construct signs. Secondly, there is the study of *codes* or *systems* into which signs are organized. This area covers the ways in which a variety of codes develop to meet the needs of a society or a culture or to exploit the channels of communication available for their transmission. Thirdly, the *culture* within which these codes and signs operate, which in turn depends on the use of these codes and signs and on their existence and the form they take, constitutes the final area of investigation.

A text, Chandler (1994) suggests, "can exist in any medium and may be verbal, non-verbal, or both", which suggests that the notion of 'text' covers advertisements which feature a critical use of images to support promotional messages. Given that semiotics defines a form of social interaction that places the individual as a member of society within the wider social spectrum, the notion of 'message' refers to the way in which a set of signs produce meanings as a direct result of their interaction with their receivers. The main emphasis is placed on how a text is read, implying that reading is a process of discovering meanings that can only occur when the individual negotiates or interacts with the text. As Fiske (1990: 3) asserts, negotiating takes place as the reader utilizes aspects of his/her own cultural experience to understand the codes and signs that make up the text.

Semiotic analysis can be applied to all text types; however, the translation of advertising texts offers a fertile area for the application of semiotic tools. From this point of view, an advertisement may be analysed as a sign which includes a number of smaller signs. Each of these signs belongs to a unique system which has its own structure and relations. Systems, or 'codes' as semioticians call them, are coherent structures consisting of signs that share similar conventions and relations. These codes can be further divided into sub-codes. The codes and sub-codes are built on the basis of existing relations between the signifiers and their referents. These relations may develop arbitrarily, as in the case of the red traffic light meaning 'stop', or on the basis of shared qualities, as in the case of a picture and the real figure in the picture. The codes and sub-codes are likely to reflect social and cultural conventions, and this will make it problematic to transfer the components of codes across different cultures. The idea of codes and sub-codes can be simply demonstrated if we take any advertisement that uses a picture of an actor or singer. In this case, there is a semiotic relationship which exists between the picture of an actor/singer and the actor/signer himself, and part of the message relies on successful access to a *cinematic* code. The cinematic code subsumes other codes such as acting, directing, singing and so on. In terms of the social context, a *social* code includes other codes such as drinking, cinemas, pubs, etc. Other codes pertaining to women, men, clothes, etc. also play a role in determining the impact of this advertisement.

Signified versus signifier

The sign is a combination of two elements: a signifier and a signified. This is how de Saussure (1916) defines the sign. The two elements are as impossible to separate from each other as the two sides of a sheet of paper. As a linguist, Saussure naturally established his semiotic model on a linguistic basis, so the definition of the sign as being composed of a signifier and a signified can only be applied to linguistic material (cf. Adab 1997: 159). In this regard, Farghal and Almanna (2015: 128) comment: "The overall meaning of a sign is primarily determined by its function within the language system as well as by its relationship with other signs used or not used".

Saussure defines the sign from a concrete vs. abstract perspective. The signifier is described as the physical form of a sign which can be touched, seen, heard, smelt or tasted, while the signified is the mental concept of the sign (cf. Farghal and Almanna 2015: 128; Bazzi 2009: 16). For example, the word *BMW*, a well-known brand of car, is a sign composed of two elements: the first is the letters B, M, W, the signifier, and the second is the mental concept to which the signifier *BMW* refers, the signified. These two constitute the written or spoken form, the sign. So, the name of the car, *BMW*, is a sign consisting of the signifier, the form of the word, and the signified, which is the mental concept existing in the user's mind. The signified is determined by what the speaker knows about the signifier. This signifier may not have a corresponding mental concept for speakers who haven't seen this car before. BMW means this particular type of car only to those who already know it, while others merely recognize it as a group of English letters. It is the relationship between the signifier and the signified which determines the meaning of a sign. This relationship is controlled by the sign user and the way s/he interprets the signifier in question.

Unlike the Peircean model (discussed in Chapter 3), the Saussurean model does not consider the object itself as an element of the sign. Saussure excludes reference to an object existing in the real world and instead restricts the relationship of reference only to the mental concept. Adab (1997: 159–160) in her critique of Saussure's model, writes:

> In stating that the description of sign function has to arise from "faits de parole" or language in use, Saussure does not, however, take into account variations in meaning which can arise from idiolect at the level of individual or of sub-group within a given socio-linguistic group (cf. Pergnier), individual intention in specific contextual use.

His definition of meaning is structural and relational rather than referential (Chandler 1994). The word 'juke-box', denoting the machine commonly used in pubs and bars to play songs chosen by the customers who pay, may be a good example here. This word is a sign consisting of the signifier, the form of the word, and the signified(s) to which this form refers in the mental world of a language user, irrespective of the real existence of such signifieds. A user of this sign may interpret it as 'song box' if the function of the object is taken into account. Another may interpret it as 'fun box' when considering it as a source of enjoyment. Some sign users may even interpret it as a 'money box', given the large amount of money it devours in return for playing songs for a few minutes. Whatever is signified is generated in the mental world of the user, the object which exists in reality does not change; it is a box placed in a bar or a pub to play songs when a specific amount of money is inserted and particular buttons are pressed by the user. The qualities of this appliance remain the same, but its mental image will vary from one person to another as discussed in Chapter 1.

According to Saussure, the relationship between a signifier and a signified is arbitrary. As a linguist, he believed that "the arbitrary nature of verbal language is the main reason for its complexity, subtlety and ability to perform a wide range of functions" (O'Sullivan et al. 1994: 288). There is thus no direct or natural relation between the signifier and the signified. The relationship between the shape of a word and the mental concept to which it refers is purely conventional. Social and cultural conventions play an essential role in determining this relationship. "The word *tree* means what it does to us only because we agree to let it do so" (Turner 1992: 13). The advertiser who intends to use a particular slogan or phrase, or even a single word, for instance, thus needs to know what conventions apply in the society and the culture of the target consumers in relation to these signs. If advertisers fail to take such conventions into consideration, the advertisement will become meaningless, with little or no impact on the intended consumers. The users of a sign are assumed to know the meanings embedded in it. Using a word or a phrase for the first time to mean something other than what people are used to will normally not generate the required relationship unless a relevant context is constructed to support the new relationship. To illustrate, the denotative meaning of the word حديقة refers to "a piece of land (usually near a house) where flowers and vegetables are grown usually with a piece of grass" (Oxford Wordpower 2010: 331). However, "more recently this word has acquired a connotative meaning in the Iraqi dialect, particularly by young people, referring to a person (male or female) who has no couple" (Almanna 2016b: 162). To put this differently, the language users have constructed a relevant context to support the new relationship between the signifier and the new signified. It usually takes a long period of time for such a relationship to become established in the social context of the users. For example, when Vodafone UK first launched their advertisements in the UK with red backgrounds, the colour 'red' meant nothing to consumers. With repeated exposure to the association between this particular colour and the advertisements

Syntagms and paradigms

Saussure defined two ways in which signs are organized into codes: syntagmatic and paradigmatic (Fiske 1990: 56). Both ways constitute a method of testing the significance of each sign and the difference between signs in terms of that significance. The two dimensions are described as two 'axes': the horizontal axis is syntagmatic, and the vertical axis is paradigmatic. Paradigms work on the principle of 'selection' while syntagms work on the principle of 'combination'. By way of explanation, the following example adapted from a short story titled: غيابات القلب الغياب الأولى الحليب *The Depths of the Heart: The First Deep: Milk* by 'Aḥmad Būzafūr (translated by and cited in Almanna and Hall 2015: 118–119) may be paid undivided attention:

اشتريت نصف لتر من الحليب، غليت الحليب في الكاصرونة، حليته بالسكر، ثم صببته في فنجان القهوة.
I buy half a liter of milk, I boil it in a saucepan and sweeten it with sugar then pour it into the coffee cup.

First, examining the original text shows how syntagmatic and paradigmatic axes constitute the micro signs that form a mental image in the mind of the hearer/reader. A paradigm is a set of signs from which the one used is chosen. In the original text, the word اشترى *to buy* is chosen from a set of possible words such as استعار *to borrow*, جلب *to bring*, سرق *to steal* and so on. The same holds true for other words used, such as:

- نصف *half* instead of ربع *quarter*, ثلث *third*, etc.
- لتر *litre* instead of بعض *some*, القليل من *little*, etc.
- حليب *milk* instead of ماء *water*, عصير *juice*, شاي *tea*, etc.
- غليت *to boil* instead of سخّن *to heat up*, etc.
- كاصرونة *saucepan* instead of إبريق *jar*, قدر *bowel*, طاوة *saucepan*, etc.
- حلّى *to sweeten* instead of خلط *to mix*, وضع *to put*, etc.
- سكّر *sugar* instead of عسل *honey*, etc.
- ثم *then* instead of بعد *after*, قبل *before*, etc.
- صبّ *to pour* instead of قدّم *to serve*, etc.
- فنجان *cup* instead of كوز *mug*, قدح *glass*, etc.
- قهوة *coffee* instead of حليب *milk*, شاي *tea*, etc.

Signs and syntagmatic and paradigmatic axes

A syntagm, on the other hand, is the linear arrangement into which the signs, which are chosen from paradigms, are combined. So the paradigmatic signs:

are combined to formulate the syntagma:

اشتريت نصف لتر من الحليب، غليت الحليب في الكاصرونة، حليته بالسكر، ثم صببته في فنجان القهوة.

Approached from a translation perspective, Almanna (2016b: 164) holds: "While translating, translators normally rely on the syntagmatic and paradigmatic axes to produce the final shape of the target text. Any change in these two axes will undoubtedly create a different mental image". Had the translators, for instance, employed different acts, such as *to bring* instead of *to buy* and *to heat up* instead of *to boil*, they would have created a mental image different from that formed by other micro signs. This clearly shows how using different syntagmatic and paradigmatic axes changes the mental image conjured up in the mind of the hearer/reader, thus affecting image resolution and translation accuracy.

To make this point clear, let us consider the following example quoted from Nathaniel Hawthorne's novel *The Scarlet Letter* (1988: 213; also discussed in Abed 2017: 93 from a different perspective), along with two translations offered by Fir'ūn (2008: 125) and 'Abū Ḥamra (2014: 246) respectively:

"Mother", said she, "was that the same minister that kissed me by the brook?"

TT1: أمي... هل كان ذلك الكاهن نفسه الذي قبلني في الغابة؟
TT2: قالت: ((أمّي! هل كان ذلك الوزير نفسه الذي قبّلني قرب الجدول؟))

In the original text, a verbal process is employed where the Sayer is *she*, *said* is the process of saying and . . . *was that the same minister that kissed me by the brook?* is the Verbiage of the process (for more details on transitivity processes, see Chapter 4 of this book). In the Verbiage, the sign *brook* is chosen from a set of possible words, such as *forest*, *river*, *tree* and the like. As can be observed, the sign *brook* has been changed to غابة *forest* in the first translation, thus creating a different mental image. However, in the second translation, it has been rendered as جدول *brook*, thereby producing a similar mental image in the minds of the target-language readers. According to formal approaches to meaning, it is the diagnostic component [+ having water] that distinguishes the lexical item جدول *brook* from the lexical item غابة *forest* [+ HAVING WATER].

In his oft-cited book *Componential Analysis of Meaning*, Nida (1975; also discussed in Almanna 2016b: 15) holds that the components of any lexeme is classified into two types, namely 'supplementary components' and 'diagnostic components'. While the former "may be very important for an extensive definition of a meaning but which are not diagnostic in specifying basic differences" (Nida 1975: 112), the latter would "specify that part of meaning that distinguishes the lexeme in question from other semantically related lexemes in a certain semantic field" (Almanna 2016b: 15).

Signifiers in a syntagm are combined to constitute a meaningful whole. Combinations in syntagms occur within a framework of syntactic rules and conventions. In language, for example, a sentence is a syntagm of words. Printed advertisements are syntagms of visual and verbal elements. Syntagms are often defined as 'sequential' and thus are temporal relationships. Some types of syntagms may represent spatial relationships, and some may represent mixed relationships (Guiraud 1975: 31). Articulated language, where signs stand in a temporal relationship to one another, is an example of the first type, the sequential. In paintings and drawings, where no sequential relationship exists among constituents, syntagmatic relations are spatial. Elements (both verbal and non-verbal) in printed advertisements are combined in such a way that they form both sequential and spatial relationships in the same advertisement.

Sequential relationships in syntagms function more clearly in screen advertising where the order of signs is important for communicating meaning. One example is an advertisement which featured Durex condoms on the Egyptian Satellite Channel (ESC) at 10pm (GMT) on 25 December 1999. It started with a man who had Arab features and was wearing the traditional white Arab robe. He consequently entered a plush bedroom, put a free telephone handset on its stand (in an upright position), took off his (expensive) gold wrist watch and walked towards the dressing table, on which there were expensive perfumes and items of make-up. A beautiful woman then came towards him, as the slogan:

which roughly means *choose carefully, choose accurately*, ended the advertisement, and the brand name Durex appeared, occupying the whole screen. Here we can distinguish two types of syntagm:

1   the syntagm: a plush room → free telephone handset → an expensive gold wrist watch → a dressing table with expensive perfumes and items of make-up → a beautiful young lady all confer on the product their own features of quality and taste that come with 'choosing carefully';
2   the syntagm: entering the bedroom → putting the free telephone handset in an upright position on its stand → taking off the wrist watch → going to the woman's dressing table connotes love making.

Other connotations can be perceived through careful selection of the elements used in the commercial. The bedroom in the Arab culture is the place where the love making usually takes place, rather than any other room in the house. The phone standing in an upright position has some phallic overtones. Taking off a wrist watch is a synecdoche (a type of metonymy) of the act of taking off clothes. There is a part-whole relationship where the part (a wrist watch) is made to represent the whole (clothes). Finally, there is going to the dressing table, which could be considered by some Arabs as a metaphor for a woman. Moreover, the advertiser successfully manages to avoid provoking cultural sensitivities by mentioning condoms directly; instead, a manipulative technique is used in which syntagmatic relationships communicate the intended meaning in a subtle way.

Paradigms, on the other hand, are sets of associated signifiers that belong to specific categories. For example, nouns and verbs are categories which are defined by grammatical rules; these categories constitute such sets from which particular items can be chosen. Langholze Leymore argues that "a sign enters into paradigmatic relations with all the signs which can also occur in the same context but not at the same time" (1975: 8). A sign of a paradigmatic set is structurally replaceable in a given context by another sign from the same set. Choosing a particular sign from a paradigmatic set shapes the preferred meaning of a text.

In advertising texts, this notion of preferred meaning can be particularly significant. To illustrate, the following advertisement (quoted from Al-Shehari 2001: 149; also discussed in Chapter 3 of this book) may be given serious consideration:

The slogan *can't start the day without one* employed in this advertisement is a good example of how syntagms and paradigms play an essential role in designing advertisement. Had the advertiser, for example, chosen the word *morning* in place of *day*, the advertisement would have been less effective. Similarly, had the word *one* been replaced by another word from the same paradigm, such as *Nescafé*, the advertisement would not have triggered the sexual connotations of *one*. The message would have lost its attractiveness, leaving the reader with only the denotative meaning produced by the word *Nescafé*.

Paradigmatic analysis helps us identify the various paradigms (sets) of signifiers which underlie the significance of the use of one signifier rather than another. Paradigmatic relationships show the oppositions and contrasts between signifiers that belong to the same paradigm and from which those signifiers used in the text were chosen. It is important to focus here on why a particular signifier rather than a workable alternative was used in a specific context, on what semioticians often refer to as 'absences'. Fiske argues that "where there is choice there is meaning, and the meaning of what was chosen is determined by the meaning of what was not" (1990: 58). Paradigmatic analysis involves comparing each of the signifiers present in the text with absent signifiers which might have been chosen in similar circumstances and considering the significance of the choices made. It can be applied at any semiotic level, from the choice of a particular word, image or sound to the choice of style, genre or medium (Fiske and Hartley 1978: 52–53). Thwaites et al. further state that factors such as technical constraints, code, convention, connotation, style, rhetorical purposes and the limitations of the individual's own repertoire influence the choice of one signifier rather than another from the same paradigm.

Deviating from the norm is one instance in which it is possible and important to identify the syntagms and the paradigms in a text. A norm is "an average example of behaviour or evaluation. It describes the common practices of a group or society and is thus *predictable*, the expected" (Fiske 1990: 101). So the unexpected and the non-conventional practices are deviations from the norm, resulting in marked choices. Normality as well as deviation can be evidenced in different degrees on a scale which starts at one end as 'very normal' and finishes at the other end as 'very deviant'. To illustrate, the following slogan adapted from an advertisement for a BRAUN shaver for women (quoted from Al-Shehari 2001: 163) is discussed here. The slogan:

يزيل . . . من جذوره

which literally means *removes . . . from its roots* is normally completed by one of a set of words with a particular set of characteristics. Elements in this paradigm have in common similar characteristics such as: something that develops, something that is physical, something that is alive. The syntagm above can be completed by one of the words from the paradigm shown here:

Normally, words like عشب *grass*, شعر *hair*, etc. can be used here to syntactically fill in the slot identified in the above slogan. This principle is known as 'slot-and-filler'

as "it tells the reader/listener the basic restrictions on the possible choices of lexical items that can be utilized by a language user to syntactically fill in every slot identified in any given text" (Almanna 2016b: 140). This figure demonstrates a rough order of deviation from the norm. The word الهمّ does not normally belong to the same paradigm to which الشجر belongs, and it is, therefore, expected to be seen in a different syntagm. Associating this element with a new set of features inserts it into another paradigm, and readers will then be encouraged to interpret it in its new syntagm. Creativity and originality, as Fiske (1990: 103) concludes, mean "breaking norms or conventions".

In an article titled 'Syntagmatic and Paradigmatic Axes as Parameters for Translation Accuracy: Towards Translating Images', Almanna (forthcoming 1) concludes that in translating literary texts:

> [I]n addition to giving full consideration to the syntagmatic and paradigmatic axes employed by the writer, issues, such as the scope of attention and intention, causation, viewing frames, pace of events, and the like should be taken into account in order to reflect an accurate mental image.

To illustrate, the following three examples will be considered here (many examples to illustrate these issues will be discussed in Chapters 6 and 7 of this book). First, the following example extracted from a short story titled الشباك والساحة *The Window and the Courtyard* by Maḥmūd ʿAbdulwahhāb (translated by and cited in Sadkhan and Pragnell 2012: 20–21) can be given full consideration:

قامت من مقعدها بهدوء، وأغلقت ضلفة الشباك اليمنى، وسارت على طرفي قدمها بحذر، ووجهها صوبه ثم أغلقت باب الغرفة وراءها.

She got up quietly from her seat, and closed the right side of the window, and tiptoed carefully, her face towards him and then closed the door behind her.

As stated above, a paradigm is a set of signs from which the one used is chosen. In the above example, four acts, namely the act of standing, the act of closing the window, the act of tiptoeing and the act of closing the room door are expressed by the writer. They are:

The act of standing up indicates that she was sitting somewhere in the room.	قامت من مقعدها بهدوء،	
The act of closing the right side of the window indicates that right side of the window was open.	أغلقت ضلفة الشباك اليمنى	و
The act of tiptoeing while her face was towards him indicates she was looking at him.	سارت على طرفي قدمها بحذر، ووجهها صوبه	و
The act of closing the room door indicates that the door was open or she opened it by herself to go out.	أغلقت باب الغرفة وراءها.	ثم

24 Signs and syntagmatic and paradigmatic axes

As can be seen, while some acts are not mentioned by the writer, i.e. they are backgrounded in attention but they can be predicted as they are in our scope of prediction, some acts are mentioned explicitly by the writer, thus foregrounding them in attention. Further, the writer, in an attempt to speed up the pace of events, opts for the additive connector و *and* twice to join the first three finite clauses. This indicates that there is no time lapse among these explicit and implicit acts. This has been given full consideration by the translators when opting for:

> *She got up quietly from her seat, and closed the right side of the window, and tiptoed carefully, her face towards him and then closed the door behind her.*

Approached from a different perspective, in the first part of this example قامت من مقعدها بهدوء، وأغلقت ضلفة الشباك اليمنى *she got up quietly from her seat, and closed the right side of the window*, the act of walking from her seat to the window is backgrounded in attention but can be easily evoked as it is in our scope of prediction. Here, open-path windowing with gapping over the medial portion of the event, that is, she walked from her seat to the window, is employed by the writer and reflected by the translators, as modelled below:

Similarly, the act of going out indicated by the phrase وراءها *behind her* is implicitly mentioned in the source text. Giving full consideration to foregrounding as opposed to backgrounding in attention, the translators have opted for an implicit act of going out, thus producing an accurate mental image.

In the following example extracted from a short story titled الشجرة المقدسة *The Sacred Tree* by Muḥammad Al-Zafzāf (translated by and cited in Husni and Newman 2008: 66–67), the emphasis in the second finite clause اختفوا *they disappeared* is put on the completion of the act of disappearing. This finite clause اختفوا *they disappeared* has been changed to a non-finite clause of purpose introduced by *in order to*. As such, the extent of causation in the original text is greater than the scope of intention as it is asserted that they disappeared. However, by the effect of *in order to*, which is used by the translators, the scope of intention becomes greater than the extent of causation, thus changing the mental image.

> أصحاب بعض الحوانيت، من خضّارين وعطارين وأشباه بقالين، تركوا سلعهم واختفوا في أماكن ما.
> *Some shopkeepers, greengrocers, spice merchants and other small traders left their goods in order to take shelter wherever they could.*

To reinforce this point, following is an example extracted from a short story titled الزر *The Button* by ʿAlī Muḥammad Al-Jaʿkī (translated by and cited in Zagood and Pragnell 2017: 8–9):

رفعت يدي بهدوء حتى يرجع خشب السرير إلى وضعه بدون ضجة. تململ قليلا وغير وضعه . . .

In these two sentences, four clauses are utilized by the writer. They are:

رفعت يدي بهدوء	It is a finite clause where the emphasis is put on the completion of the act of raising his hand quietly.
حتى يرجع خشب السرير إلى وضعه بدون ضجة	It is a non-finite clause of purpose introduced by حتى *in order to*.
تململ قليلا	It is a finite clause where the emphasis is placed on the completion of the act of fidgeting.
وغيّر وضعه	It is a finite clause where the emphasis is put on the completion of the act of changing position.

Apart from the non-finite clause حتى يرجع خشب السرير إلى وضعه بدون ضجة, the extent of causation in the three finite clauses is greater than the scope of intention. This is because it is asserted that he raised his hand, fidgeted a little and changed his position. Further, in these three finite clauses, the described acts are approached from a distal perspective (for more details on perspectival systems, see Chapter 7 of this book); therefore, the three acts are reduced to be seen as three points on the timeline, as modelled below:

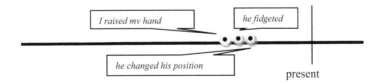

By contrast, the scope of intention in the non-finite clause of purpose introduced by حتى *in order to* is greater than the extent of causation. Being fully aware of the grammatical forms utilized by the writer, the translators have produced an accurate translation where the emphasis is also put on the completion of the acts.

> *I quietly raised my hand to allow the bed to settle back without making a sound. He fidgeted a little and changed his position . . .*

Commutation test

Some semioticians refer to the concept of a 'commutation test' which can be used in order to identify distinctive signifiers and to define their significance. To apply this test, a particular signifier in a text is selected, then alternatives to this signifier are considered. The effects of each substitution are considered in terms of how it might affect the sense made of the overall sign. This might involve imagining the use of a coloured shot rather than a black-and-white one; a substitution in sex, age, language or dialect; and substituting models. The influence of the substitution on the overall meaning can help suggest the contribution of the original signifier and also identify syntagmatic units (Fiske and Hartley 1978: 54–55; Barthes 1985: 19–20; Fiske 1990: 109–110; Al-Shehari 2001: 166).

The commutation test can identify the paradigms (the sets) to which the signifiers used to belong. In an Arabic advertisement that employs a deer, for instance, when the deer is changed into another animal and, accordingly, the meaning is changed, this animal is then a member of the paradigm; the paradigm set for it would consist of all of those alternative signifiers which could have been used and which would have changed the meaning. Thwaites et al. (1994: 41) offer these examples:

> Does a bottle of cheap red wine carry the same meaning as a French vintage? What would it mean to eat your dessert first? Does an evening gown mean the same thing regardless of whether it's worn by a man or a woman?

In advertising photographs, the choice of a particular object or person with a particular image, focus or colour is done deliberately. The advertiser tries to deliver a particular meaning or effect to the consumer; to do so, s/he tries to choose a specific size and type of font, a special focus of the image and even a particular person or type of person. Changing these elements would change the overall meaning and impact of the advertisement. Inserting a setting element into an advertisement from another paradigm of setting elements is one of the attractive methods used commonly by professional advertisers. By way of explanation, the following advertisement for a beer called ستيلا *Stella* can be given adequate consideration. In this advertisement, a film-promotion setting is used instead of the normal advertising setting showing the product, logo, slogan, headings and a text. Borrowing a new context or setting to promote a product motivates the reader to continue reading the advertisement. To make this point clear, the advertisement for a beer called سقارة *Saqāra* can be considered. The normal expected advertising setting for promoting this product might start with a heading, followed by photos of the product and someone drinking it, a slogan, text and perhaps a logo. This is the norm, but what can be observed in this advertisement is something that deviates from the norm. The setting is borrowed from another paradigm which is normally used to promote newly launched newspapers or magazines. The advertisement starts with the heading:

الأن بالأسواق

roughly meaning *now on the market*. This is normally seen as a heading in an advertisement for a new newspaper or magazine, especially if الأسواق *markets* is replaced by الأكشاك *kiosks*. The form within which the depicted product is placed is that of a magazine with the same title as the product being advertised, written in a large, white font at the top.

The features and the selling points of the product are presented in the form of headlines displaying the contents of the magazine, placed on the right-hand side of the product. The text below repeats the headlines within the border. It starts with the heading:

داخل هذا العدد

meaning *inside this issue*, in a large, red font to emphasize the nature of the borrowed setting, as if it is promoting a new magazine. The features of the product then follow in the colours 'white' and 'yellow' as headlines of reports about the product.

This advertisement also borrows features from a paradigm other than that relating to promoting magazines, namely the paradigm of poetry. This can be seen in the way in which the headlines, or the features of the product, are written. They are all written in the form of rhymes, with each headline consisting of two parts, both ending with the same pattern:

سقارة ممتازة لمّت الحبايب ومخلتش حد غايب

The words الحبايب and غايب share the same final pattern ايب to create a rhythmic effect. Another creative technique in this advertisement comes from the successful choice of the colour 'yellow' for the border around the product. This particular colour denotes the real colour of the product, yellow. Secondly, 'bright yellow' can suggest fun, youth, and freedom. The advertiser is cleverly trying to associate such meanings with buying the product.

To sum up, the meaning of any message is constituted through a network of relationships, either between its signs or with signs that exist outside it. To test the significance of each sign used in a given text and the difference between signs in terms of that significance, syntagmatic and paradigmatic axes as two dimensions working on two different principles, that is, the principle of selection (paradigms) and the principle of combination (syntagms), can be used. It has been shown that to create an accurate mental image in the mind of the target-language reader, the translator, in addition to giving full consideration to the syntagmatic and paradigmatic axes, needs to pay extra attention to issues such as the scope of intention, extend of causation, windowing of attention, pace of events and the like. In advertising texts, the choice of a particular object or person with a particular image, focus or colour is done deliberately.

28 Signs and syntagmatic and paradigmatic axes

A particular meaning or effect is intended to be delivered by the advertisers to the consumers, hence their choice between different sizes and types of font, colours, layouts and even different people and objects. Therefore, changing any element would result in a different meaning and impact of the advertisement. Inserting, for instance, a setting element into an advertisement from another paradigm of setting elements would change the overall meaning and impact. With this in mind, this technique has become one of the attractive methods commonly used by professional advertisers.

Key technical terms

- Commutation test
- Diagnostic components
- Extent of causation
- Metonymy
- Pace of events
- Paradigm
- Paradigmatic axis
- Scope of intention
- Semiotics
- Sign
- Signified
- Signifier
- Slot-and-filler principle
- Structural semiotics
- Supplementary components
- Synecdoche
- Syntagm
- Syntagmatic axis
- Windowing of attention

Exercises

Exercise 1: The following text is extracted from a short story titled الزر *The Button* by ʿAlī Muḥammad Al-Jaʿkī (translated by and cited in Zagood and Pragnell (2017: 6–7). Comment on the translation accuracy by touching on issues, such as the scope of intention, extend of causation and pace of events.

I was looking at him through a small gap between the folds of my blanket, without making any movement that could show that I was awake.	كنت أراقبه من خلال فرجة صغيرة بين ثنايا اللحاف، دون أن أقوم بحركة تنبئ عن يقظتي...
He lay on his back, facing the ceiling and closed his eyes.	استقر على ظهره مواجها السقف، وأغمض عينيه...
I waited a little, and then I made some noise.	انتظرت قليلا وأحدثت صوتا...
His eyes didn't blink and his face didn't twitch.	لم تطرف عيناه، ولم ترتعش تقاسيم وجهه...

Exercise 2: Use the syntagmatic and paradigmatic axes to see the strength of the relationship between these two *BBC* news items (30 November 2014; also discussed in Almanna 2016a: 201–202):

An investigation into corruption in the Iraqi army has revealed that there were 50,000 false names on its payroll.	كشف تحقيق أجرته الحكومة العراقية في شأن الفساد بالجيش أن هناك 50 ألف ((جندي شبح)) في قائمة الرواتب التي تدفعها الحكومة العراقية لقواتها.

Exercise 3: Translate the following text extracted from *BBC* (1 November 2017), then annotate your own translation, focusing on the syntagmatic and paradigmatic axes.

قتل ثمانية أشخاص على الأقل وأصيب 12 آخرون عندما اقتحم سائق شاحنة طريقا مخصصا للمشاة وراكبي الدراجات الهوائية في حي مانهاتن بمدينة نيويورك. وأطلقت الشرطة النار على رجل في التاسعة والعشرين حين خروجه من السيارة وألقت القبض عليه. وقالت وسائل الإعلام الأمريكية إن الرجل يدعى سيف الله سايبوف، وهو مهاجر قدم إلى الولايات المتحدة عام 2010. وأشارت وسائل الإعلام إلى أنه يعيش في فلوريدا.

Exercise 4: The following extract is taken from a speech delivered by US President Barack Obama at the Opening Session of the 70th United Nations General Assembly at the United Nations Headquarters in New York City on 27 December 2015. His speech has been translated into Arabic by Al-Jazeera and RT Arabic, respectively (cited in Mzaiel 2017: 90). Use the syntagmatic and paradigmatic axes to see the strong relationship between the ST and each TT.

ST: *We're told that such retrenchment is required to beat back disorder; that it's the only way to stamp out terrorism, or prevent foreign meddling.*

TT1: يقال لنا إن هذا مطلب لكي نكافح الإرهاب و لكي نحول دون تدخل الدول الأجنبية . . .

TT2: يقولون إن ذلك أمر مهم ولازم للقضاء على الإرهاب والفوضى. فهم أيضا . . . يدعون إلى الحيلولة دون تدخل الأطراف الجانبية . . .

Excercise 5: In the following example quoted from Nathaniel Hawthorne's novel *The Scarlet Letter* (1988: 213), the lexical item *minister* has been translated by Firʿūn (2008: 125) into كاهن and by 'Abū Ḥamra (2014: 246) into وزير. Identify the diagnostic component that distinguishes the lexical item كاهن from وزير.

ST: *"Mother", said she, "was that the same minister that kissed me by the brook?"*

TT1: أمي... هل كان ذلك هو الكاهن نفسه الذي قبلني في الغابة؟

TT2: قالت: ((أَمّي! هل كان ذلك الوزير نفسه الذي قبّلني قرب الجدول؟))

Further reading

Almanna, A. (2016a). *The Routledge Course in Translation Annotation: Arabic-English-Arabic*. London/New York: Routledge.

——. (2016b). *Semantics for Translation Students: Arabic-English-Arabic*. Oxford: Peter Lang.

Al-Shehari, K. (2001). *The Semiotics and Translation Advertising Texts: Conventions, Constraints and Translation Strategies with Particular Reference to English and Arabic*, unpublished Ph.D. thesis: University of Manchester.

Bazzi, S. (2009). *Arab News and Conflict*. Amsterdam/Philadelphia, PA: John Benjamins Publishing Company.

Blonsky, M. (ed.) (1985). *On Signs – A Semiotic Reader*. Oxford: Basil Blackwell.

Faiq, S. and Sabry, R. (2013). "Altered Semiotics Through Translation", *Sayyab Translation Journal*, Vol. 5, pp. 45–56.

Farghal, M. and Almanna, A. (2015). *Contextualizing Translation Theories: Aspects of Arabic-English Interlingual Communication*. Newcastle upon Tyne: Cambridge Scholars Publishing.

Grutman, R. (2009). "Multilingualism". In M. Baker and G. Saldanha (eds.), *Routledge Encyclopedia of Translation Studies* (2nd edn), pp. 182–185. London/New York: Routledge.
Hatim, B. and Mason, I. (1990). *Discourse and the Translator*. London: Longman.
Pertilli, S. (1992). "Translation, Semiotics and Ideology", *TTR: Traduction, Terminologie, Redaction*, Vol. 5 (1), pp. 233–264.
Saussure, F. de (1916/1983). *Cours de linguistique générale*. Paris: Editions Payot, trans. by R. Harris (1983) as *Course in General Linguistics*. London: Duckworth.

References

Abed, M. A. (2017). *Evaluating Three Translations of Nathaniel Hawthorne's Novel the Scarlet Letter into Arabic: A Pragmatic Approach*, unpublished M.A. thesis: Basrah University.
'Abū Ḥamra, A. (2014). الحرف القرمزي (trans.) Beirut: Dār Al-Ḥikāyāt.
Adab, B. J. (1997). *Translation Strategies and Cross-Cultural Constraints: A Case Study of the Translation of Advertising Texts*, unpublished Ph.D. thesis: Aston University.
Almanna, A. (2016a). *The Routledge Course in Translation Annotation: Arabic-English-Arabic*. London/New York: Routledge.
———. (2016b). *Semantics for Translation Students: Arabic-English-Arabic*. Oxford: Peter Lang.
———. (forthcoming 1). "Syntagmatic and Paradigmatic Axes as Parameters for Translation Accuracy: Towards Translating Images".
Almanna, A. and Hall, M. (2015; bilingual edn). *Moroccan Short Stories: A Bilingual Reader*. München: Lincom Europa Academic Publishers.
Al-Shehari, K. (2001). *The Semiotics and Translation Advertising Texts: Conventions, Constraints and Translation Strategies with Particular Reference to English and Arabic*, unpublished Ph.D. thesis: University of Manchester.
Barthes, R. (1985). *The Fashion System* (translated by Matthew Ward and Richard Howard). London: Jonathan Cape.
Bazzi, S. (2009). *Arab News and Conflict*. Amsterdam/Philadelphia, PA: John Benjamins Publishing Company.
Blonsky, M. (ed.) (1985). *On Signs – A Semiotic Reader*. Oxford: Basil Blackwell.
Chandler, D. (1994). *Semiotics for Beginners*. <www.aber.ac.uk/-dgc/semiotic.html>
Faiq, S. and Sabry, R. (2013). "Altered Semiotics Through Translation", *Sayyab Translation Journal*, Vol. 5, pp. 45–56.
Farghal, M. and Almanna, A. (2015). *Contextualizing Translation Theories: Aspects of Arabic-English Interlingual Communication*. Newcastle upon Tyne: Cambridge Scholars Publishing.
Fir'ūn, M. T. (trans.) (2008). الحرف القرمزي. Damascus: Dār 'Usāma.
Fiske, J. (1990). *Introduction to Communication Studies*. London: Routledge.
Fiske, J. and Hartley, J. (1978). *Reading Television*. London: Methuen.
Grutman, R. (2009). "Multilingualism". In M. Baker and G. Saldanha (eds.), *Routledge Encyclopedia of Translation Studies* (2nd edn), pp. 182–185. London/New York: Routledge.
Guiraud, P. (1975). *Semiology* (translated by George Gross). London: Routledge and Kegan Paul.
Hatim, B. and Mason, I. (1990). *Discourse and the Translator*. London: Longman.
Hawthorne, N. (1988). *The Scarlet Letter*. Beirut: York Press.
Husni, R. and Newman, D. (2008; bilingual edn). *Modern Arabic Short Stories: A Binigual Reader*. London: Saqi Books.
Langholz Leymore, V. (1975). *Hidden Myth: Structure and Symbolism in Advertising*. New York: Basic Books.
Nida, E. A. (1975). *Componential Analysis of Meaning*. The Hague: Mouton.

Nöth, W. (1990). *Handbook of Semiotics*. Bloomington: Indiana University Press.
O'Sullivan, T., Hartley, J., Saunders, D., Montgomery, M. and Fiske, J. (1994). *Key Concepts in Communicationa and Cultural Studies*. London: Routledge.
Oxford Wordpower. (2010). Oxford: Oxford University Press.
Pertilli, S. (1992). "Translation, Semiotics and Ideology", *TTR: Traduction, Terminologie, Redaction*, Vol. 5 (1), pp. 233–264.
Sadkhan, R. and Pragnell, F. (2012). رائحة الشتاء *The Scent of Winter: A Bilingual Reader*. London: Sayyab Books Ltd.
Saussure, F. de (1916/1983). *Cours de linguistique générale*. Paris: Editions Payot, trans. by R. Harris (1983) as *Course in General Linguistics*. London: Duckworth.
Stam, R., Burgoyne, R. and Flitterman-Lewis, S. (1992). *New Vocabularies in Film Semiotics: Structuralism, Post-Structuralism and Beyond*. London: Routledge.
Thwaites, T., Davis, L. and Mules, W. (1994). *Tools for Cultural Studies: An Introduction*. South Melbourne: Macmillan.
Turner, G. (1992). *British Cultural Studies: An Introduction*. New York: Routledge.
Zagood, M. and Pragnell, F. (2017; bilingual edn). أموت كلّ يوم *I Die Every Day*. München: Lincom Europa Academic Publishers.

3
A SIGN'S FUNCTIONS AND INTERTEXTUALITY

In the previous chapter, issues such as signs, signifiers, signifieds and syntagmatic and paradigmatic axes were discussed in a direct link with the actual act of translation. Syntagmatic and paradigmatic axes were used as parameters to test the significance of the sign and, accordingly, the translation accuracy. In this chapter, the sign's functions (be it iconic, indexical or symbolic) are given full consideration. In addition to these three main functions, the intertextual relationships established between the set of signs are discussed in a direct link with translation.

Peirce's interpretive semiotics

Like Saussure (1916/83), Peirce (1931) focuses on explaining the relationship between the sign and the thought it evokes, but unlike Saussure, he builds into his theory a reference to external reality. For Peirce, thought is the mediator between a sign and its signified:

> A representamen is that character of a thing by virtue of which, for the production of a certain mental effect, it may stand in place of another thing. The thing having this character I term a representamen, the mental effect, or thought, its interpretant, the thing for which it stands, its object.
>
> *(CP 1, 564)*

Here, Peirce suggests that the sign starts from the representamen, that is, the form of the sign (whether written or spoken), which provokes a mental concept, the interpretant, about the object to which it refers. Peirce explains that "a sign is something, A, which denotes some fact or object, B, to some interpretant thought, C" (CP 1, 346).

Peirce thus assumes a three-way relationship between the sign, the user and external reality. Peirce's triangle begins by addressing a sign to somebody, who creates, through knowledge and experience, an equivalent sign known as the interpretant in his/her own mind. This interpretant stands for something outside the user, called the object.

For example, the word أوباما *Obama*, used in the Iraqi dialect, is a sign which creates an equivalent interpretant in the user's mind, which is a mental concept referring to a particular type of car in the real world, i.e. a Dodge Charger. The user's pre-knowledge about such a model allows him/her to interpret أوباما *Obama* as a car. Similarly, the lexical item مونيكا *Monika* used in Yemen refers to a particular type of car in the real world, i.e. a Land Cruiser. Any sign can produce two kinds of meaning: denotative and connotative. The denotative meaning is the literal (direct) meaning that can be understood via a direct and clear relationship between the sign and the thing to which it refers. The connotative meanings, on the other hand, are those which come into existence as a result of an interaction between the sign and the user's context. By way of explanation, let us discuss the meaning of the lexical item *dog*. The denotative or literal meaning of *dog* is "an animal that many people keep as a pet, or for working on farms, hunting, etc. [it] can bark, growl, whine and wag" (*Oxford Wordpower Dictionary* 2006: 232). However, the word also brings to mind a number of associations (i.e. connotations or shades of meanings) such as 'fidelity' in some cultures. For Arabs, the word *dog*, in addition to referring to a physical referent in the real world (denotation), it invokes in the mind of the hearer/reader the concept of fidelity (connotation). So, the relationship between the denotative meaning and the connotative meaning is what Peirce calls 'interpretant' that works as a sign, as modelled below:

however, "while the physical referent has not changed, its interpretant has drastically changed in Standard Arabic and all Arabic vernaculars where the association is now between the object *dog* and meanness/contempt" (Farghal and Almanna 2015: 151). Another interesting example is the word اِشرد currently used in the Iraqi dialect, especially by young people, which means *handsome, beautiful, breathtaking*, etc. (connotation), in addition to its literal, straightforward meaning *escape* (denotation) (for more examples, see Almanna 2016b: 154–155).

This interaction occurs between the sign and everything related to the user, including pre-knowledge about the relevant sign: the emotions, feelings, culture to which the user has access, etc. (Fiske 1990: 86). According to Peirce, the term 'connotation' can be further sub-divided into three kinds of signs:

1   *iconic* sign, as one that resembles the signified,
2   *indexical* sign, having associations and inherent connections with the signified, and
3   *symbolic* sign, having no resemblance with the signified, and the connotation is learnt.

Peirce further differentiates between the sign and its functions. According to him, there are three types of functions, namely iconic, indexical and symbolic. Farghal and Almanna (2015) link these three functions of the sign to the translation process. They hold (p. 130–1):

> In order to understand a sign, which functions in the first place iconically, translators sometimes do '*intralingual*' translation, to use Jakobson's (1959/1992: 145) classification, in an attempt to determine the sign's indexical function. If the translator fails to find a TL sign with a similar iconic function, then s/he relies on the indexical function of the sign to arrive by paraphrasing, expansion and so on at a somewhat different sign in terms of iconicity. It is worth noting here that the iconicity of the sign, i.e. the relation between a sign and its object, "is not wholly established by rules, by a code, as in the case of symbols", and "does not preexist with respect to the code, as in the case of indexes, but rather is invented freely and creatively" by virtue of the relation established between a particular object in the real world and what this object invokes in the mind of the hearer/reader (Pertilli 1992: 240).
> (Farghal and Almanna 2015: 130–1)

These three functions, that is, iconic function, indexical function and symbolic function, are given serious consideration here.

Iconic function

An icon is a sign used to describe, mentally or visually, something similar to the signified (e.g. a photograph, a computer icon, a road sign, a diagram, a map) (Adab 1997: 298). In a similar vein, an icon has been referred to as "a sign which refers to the object that it denotes merely by virtue of characters of its own" (CP 2, 247). Taking such definitions into consideration, it can be stated that such a sign is suitable for presenting anything with a corresponding set of features. Icons thus share characteristics with what they represent, usually in a direct way (i.e. when a colour sample is an icon for the paint in a specific paint pot, or a relief map is an icon for a country). In terms of Peirce's semiotics, when we use a relief map to study the properties of a country, we exploit a property of the sign, which it would have had even if its object had not existed. This is possible because of an isomorphism between the map and the country: there is a correspondence between properties each could have had, whatever the character of the other. A relief map can thus provide us with information about the country it represents. For instance, given an understanding of the geographical conventions, measurements and drawings on the map, a map provides us with information about the hills, valleys, rivers, etc. in that country.

By way of explanation, the advertisement which appeared in *Marie Claire* (also discussed in Al-Shehari 2001: 125) about FREEDOM fragrance for men and women may be considered here. In the advertisement, a number of interesting examples of the way in which an iconic relationship between signs can be established by the use of images. The iconic relationship in this advertisement exists in two parallel directions:

a   between elements in the advertisement and their signifieds in reality, and
b   between elements in the advertisement and their signifieds in the same advertisement.

In the first case, iconic relationships exist between the image of the product and the actual bottles of FREEDOM in reality, between the picture of the American flag and the actual flag and between the people in the picture and real people. Irrespective of the symbolic relations that may exist here (especially in relation to the flag), the iconic relationships established in the advertisement may help the reader interpret the meanings that the advertiser intends to convey in relation to the product. The overall image of a crowd holding the American flag and aspiring to freedom, led by one or two people, iconically reminds the reader of the real events surrounding the declaration of independence in the USA. This image, in turn, will bring to the consumer's mind such messages as enthusiasm, power, independence, and freedom. In other words, the message is: if you buy this product, you will achieve all these positive things.

Arabic advertisements tend to rely less heavily on manipulating iconic relationships. A good example is an Arabic advertisement about a شماغ *shimāgh*, which is a piece of cloth worn on the head or around the shoulders by Arabs (mainly men) in the Arabian Peninsula and some other Arab regions. This product is manufactured in London, but only for Arabs; the advertisement is thus meant only for Arabs.

It is worth mentioning that these Arabic advertisements about this product are most likely typical in that it does not invite consumers to think beyond the surface message. It simply invites them to buy the product depicted. There is no attempt to manipulate images or even words. The advertiser could have easily found other ways of promoting the product to engage the reader more fully, such as picturing a film star wearing the *shimāgh*.

Indexical function

An index is a sign that suggests a fact or state of affairs (e.g. dark clouds can indicate rain, smoke usually indicates fire). It is a sign which is inherently linked in some way, existentially or causally, to the signified (e.g. barometer, weathercock, knock on door). The existential link between an index and an object functions by virtue of directing the attention of the interpreter to the object of the sign (e.g. calendar, weather vane) so that it provides information about that object without mentioning it. An index is "a sign which refers to the object that it denotes by virtue of being really affected by that object" (CP 2, 248). That is, there is a dyadic natural relation between sign and object which is independent of our practices. Thus, smoke is an index of fire and low barometric pressure is an index of impending rain, irrespective of various cultural practices or beliefs.

To demonstrate how the indexical function of a sign works, let us consider these two advertisements. To begin with, the advertisement about Fairy washing powder, which appeared in *OK!*, may be considered. Fairy is associated in most advertisements with the image of a 'baby'. The image of the 'baby' appearing on Fairy packets is used to promote the product. Here, an implicit message is sent out to the customers that Fairy is the product that helps make your clothes soft. This implicit message is characterized by having a force-dynamic value to make your clothes, which were dirty, soft and clean. This force-dynamic framework enables us to capture the causing (the use of Fairy) of the expected result (your clothes will be soft and clean). For more details on force dynamics, see Chapter 7 of this book.

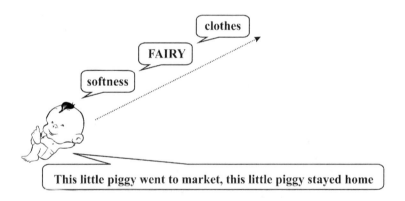

The idea of softness is transferred from the natural softness of a baby's skin. Baby clothes get dirty faster than those of adults because of the nature of a baby's bodily functions, thus Fairy is effective even with the clothes of babies. We could go on exploring other potential indexical relationships triggered by the association between Fairy and babies. In some products, the notion of babyhood is indexically represented by the inclusion of a variant of a line from a nursery rhyme, which is well known by children and widely sung in English nurseries: "This little piggy

A sign's functions and intertextuality 37

went to market, this little piggy stayed home [...]". This rhyme is usually accompanied by folding down each of the child's five toes, then the adult's fingers move lightly along the child's leg to cause laughter. Another indexical relationship exists between the word 'piggy' and the notion of childhood. 'Piggy' is widely used in the UK as a term of endearment, perhaps for a naughty child, and more particularly for a child who eats a lot of chocolate. Chocolate is particularly difficult to wash off clothes, and this may conceivably provide another indirect indexical link in the advertisement.

Now, let us discuss the following advertisement, which is about an Arabic newspaper called الشرق الأوسط *Al-Sharq Al-'Awsaṭ*, promoted in *Al-Jadīda* (quoted from Al-Shehari 2001: 131). This advertisement features less successful manipulation of indexical relationships. The letterbox in the advertisement is a sign that carries several meanings simultaneously. It indicates a particular culture and set of postal practices. Not all countries use a postal system in which mail is delivered to homes through holes fixed in doors. In some countries, postal boxes are placed outside houses for this purpose. In other countries, as in some Arab countries like Yemen, Sudan, Iraq, Oman and the like, the only way to receive post is through post boxes at the post office. Therefore, the letterbox in this advertisement functions as an index to the postal delivery service in some countries but not in others. Apart from the postal function, another indexical relationship exists with 'timing'. The time associated with delivering post through a personal letterbox is normally early morning. The letterbox in the advertisement therefore indexically suggests 'early morning'. Picturing the advertised newspaper already in a letterbox implies efficiency in terms of delivering it to your door early in the morning. The advertiser strengthens this meaning with the slogan at the bottom:

which literally means 'a successful newspaper does not yawn'. Including the verb *to yawn* in the slogan brings to mind the concept of 'time', implying early morning. Since this newspaper is promoted as 'not yawning', the reader will associate with it such meanings as punctuality, reliability, speed of delivery and quality. The basis for such interpretations is the indexical relationship which exists between 'letterbox' and 'early morning'. Arabs who are not familiar with the postal system in question may not perceive this relationship. This raises the question of the effectiveness of this picture in such an advertisement. Peirce's relationships are based on an interaction between the sign, the object and the user so that resulting meanings (for Peirce) are communicated irrespective of the situational context in which such a sign exists. For instance, a footprint which looks like that of a man indicates the existence of a man (indexical) and a picture of a tiger refers to a real tiger (iconic). Social semioticians, on the other hand, examine semiotic practices specific to a particular culture and context in order to understand how various meanings are communicated in various situational contexts (Halliday 1976; Hodge and Kress 1988). This social branch of semiotics allows for a wider range of interpretations of the sign than Peirce's theory. Every human being may interpret a particular sign in a different way based on his or her life experiences. Robinson Crusoe, for instance, considers the footprint which he sees on the sand to be that of the devil, although he describes it as exactly the footprint of a man. It is the harshness of the situation in which Crusoe finds himself and the fact that he has no contact with any human beings that lead him to interpret the footprint as that of a devil. Trying to find a rational interpretation for the existence of such a footprint, Crusoe later thinks that this foot may belong to a wild savage who lives in the area. Later still, after reciting some verses from the Bible, he feels more cheerful and tries to convince himself that the footstep belongs to him. Thus three different interpretations of the same sign can be reached by the same person in three different contexts, whereas, in Peircean terms, there can only be one indexical interpretation for such a footprint, i.e. as a sign indicating the presence of a human being. Moreover, according to social semioticians even with iconic relationships which are based on similarities between the signifier and its signified, interpretation still remains open. If a picture of a tiger is shown to someone who has never seen a tiger before, the tiger may be interpreted as something else, probably the closest animal to the one depicted.

To sum up, social semiotics, a synthesis of contemporary approaches to the social production of meaning, is based on mainstream semiotics, a theoretical approach to the study of signs and sign systems. Semiotics can also be considered more generally as the study of meaning, its central concern being how meanings are generated. Social semiotics takes this concern in a particular direction. As the term suggests, it focuses on social interaction: on how people construct meaning, rather than on the meanings themselves. The central notion of social semiotics is that all meanings are made. They do not exist as objects or concrete facts. Rather, they are constructed through systems of signs. Meaning relations cannot be understood outside of their use in the social practices of some community (Lemke 1987: 218). Meanings are made through the social practices which construct semiotic relations among forms, ideas, material processes, entities and social actions. A given community or sub-community has regular patterns of interpretation which are the outcome of cultural and historical factors. For example, committing adultery leads (perhaps indexically) to hell in Arab and Islamic societies but not in other societies. The same differences exist with regards to the shape of the earth, which was once thought to be flat but is now believed to be spherical. The difference between traditional semiotics and social semiotics is particularly important to spell out in the context of discussing

Symbolic function

The term 'symbol' is used to describe an arbitrary or totally conventional relationship between the sign and the object for which it stands (e.g. the word 'peach' conventionally stands for the fruit we associate with the word) (Adab 1997: 298). Further examples include, for instance, the word 'stop', or a red traffic light, indicating that drivers must bring vehicles to a halt. The symbol is "a sign which is constituted merely or mainly by the fact that it is used and understood as such" (CP 2, 307). This means that the phonetic alphabet of a particular language is made up of symbols which correspond to the various sounds that make up the language. Phonetic signs do not exploit any resemblance between the symbols and the sounds, nor is there a natural causal relation between the symbols and the sounds. Instead there is a general practice of using the symbols for this purpose, and they are symbols by virtue of this convention.

Symbolic relationships need to be either learnt or agreed on by convention so that they can be understood. Colours, for example are not used by people "haphazardly, but rather symbolically, depending on the impressions or feelings each colour may arouse in souls" (Sadkhan 2010: 74). He adds:

> Though colour symbolism is looked upon differently by different cultures and peoples, human beings seem to have a oneness in experiencing colour expressions, with relative differences among mankind. This relativity accounts for the fact that 'each individual sees, feels, and evaluates colour in a very personal way' (Itten 1961: 13) [...] The ability to use colour symbolically or literally is linked to one's language. As such, colours are terms that express concepts to communicate certain messages.

For instance, the colour *black* signifies mourning in the Arab as well as the Western Worlds, but the colour *white* has the same signification in China. As such, the translators need to be careful when dealing with colour terms as they sometimes lose their colourness when being translated into another language/culture (for more details, see Sadkhan 2010: 73–92). By way of explanation, let us consider the following examples:

English	*Arabic*	*Back-translation*
• Black and white thinker	مفكّر متزمت	*Extremist thinker*
• Black Friday	جمعة حزينة	*Sad Friday*
• To look black	ينظر شزرا	*To look angrily*
• Black look	نظرة غضبى أو غاضبة	*Angry look*

English	Arabic	Back-translation
• Blue moon	بعيد جدا أو نادر جدا	Very far or rare
• Blue film	فلم إباحي	Pornographic film
• To blue money	ينفق بإسراف	To spend a lot of money
• Blue jokes	نكات بذيئة	Improper jokes
• Blue laws	قوانين إنفاقية	Sumptuary laws
• To show white feather	خاف/جبن	To be afraid or frightened
• To be yellow	خاف/جبن	To be afraid or frightened
• Blue murder	موت أحمر	Red death
• Yellow press	الصحافة الرخيصة	Press abounding in exaggerated, sensational articles
• White night	ليلة مسهّدة	Sleepless night
• White-handed	طاهر اليدين	Having hands unstained with guilt
• Red-handed	بالجرم المشهود/متلبّس بالجريمة	Being caught in the crime scene
• Green-eyed	غيور/حسود	Jealous

In the following list, however, both languages map and conceptualize the socio-cultural experiences in a similar way, thus resulting in optimal equivalence where both formal and functional equivalents coincide (Farghal 2012: 47; Almanna 2016b: 165).

English	Arabic	Back-translation
• Black comedy	الكوميديا السوداء	Black comedy
• Black market	السوق السوداء	Black market
• Black and white television	تلفزيون أبيض وأسود	White and black television
• White lie	كذبة بيضاء	White lie
• Green zone	المنطقة الخضراء	Green zone
• White flag	الراية البيضاء	White flag

To make this point clear, the following example extracted from a novel titled ثرثرة فوق النيل *Adrift on the Nile* by Mahfouz (1966: 30) and translated by Liardet (1993: 10) may be considered:

ضبطته يغازل جارة جديدة!
يا خبر أحمر...
ولعلع صوتي حتى سمعه سابع جار!

She puffed voraciously and said, to satisfy the curiosity around her: "I caught him flirting with the new neighbor!"
Salacious news!
And I should think they heard me on the seventh floor!

There are two signs that need special treatment, viz. يا خبر أحمر and سابع جار. Semiotically speaking, both recall other signs which refer to the same referents. To begin with the first sign, in Egypt and some other countries, يا خبر أحمر lit. *Oh what red news!* (also يا خبر أبيض *Oh, what white news* or just ياخبر *Oh what news!*) is used by people when hearing bad or strange news. Having paid extra attention to the overall image along with its micro signs' functions on the one hand, and given full consideration to the linguistic and stylistic norms of the TL, the translator has resorted to replacing the colour term أحمر *red* with another term, i.e. *salacious*. Being fully aware that some colour terms may lose their colourness while being transferred from one language/culture into another, the translator has opted for a functional equivalent, that is, undivided attention is given to the function of the SL expression, independently of the form and its image conjured up in the mind of the SL reader, thus guaranteeing acceptability, naturalness and readability (Almanna 2016a: 41).

The second sign that needs special treatment is the expression سابع جار *the seventh neighbour*. In an attempt to inject his text with vividness and make it more influential, the writer opts for building an intertextual relation with a religious sentence commonly used by Arabs, that is, النبي وصّى على سابع جار *The prophet recommends that we take care of the seventh neighbour*, thus transferring a set of religious signs to his text. The Islamic religion cares a lot about neighbours; it recommends everyone to be kind to his/her neighbours and not bother them in any way. The Prophet Muhammad (peace be upon him) said: "Whoever believes in God and the Last Day should be generous to his neighbor" (Al-Muwatta, n.y. Volume 49, Hadith 22). Here, in this context, the religious expression is used to indicate the reaction of the lady whose louder voice was heard for a long distance. Insisting on reflecting the lexical item سابع *seventh*, the translator has opted for the lexical item *floor* rather than *neighbour*, thus creating a mental image that gives the vertical axis a front seat at the expense of both the horizontal axis and the issue of taking care of neighbours. The lexical item سابع *seventh* is just a component of a unitary sign, as it does not have a pragmatic and communicative value in this context according to Arab culture, thus failing to recall another signifier by itself.

To reinforce this, the following example quoted from Mahfouz's (1973: 40) novel اللص والكلاب *The Thief and the Dogs* and translated by Adel Ata Elyas (1987: 118) can be given full consideration:

وثمة رائحة سحرية لا تصدر إلا من دم أزرق رغم أنفه المائل إلى الفطس.

He felt a magic scent in the air, something he couldn't identify in spite of his long sharp nose. It was the smell of aristocracy.

In this example, the expression that needs to be given full consideration is دم أزرق *blue blood*. For a native speaker of Arabic, this expression, that is, دم ازرق "recalls another signifier, a person of aristocratic or wealthy ancestry, which refers to the same signified" (Almanna 2016b: 165). To put this differently, this expression, in addition to referring to a physical referent in the real world, evokes in our mind the "the image of a person of aristocratic or wealthy ancestry, thus creating a relationship (interpretant) between blue blood and a person of aristocratic or wealthy ancestry" (Ibid.). As can be observed, the translator has opted for the word 'aristocracy' where he has turned a blind eye to the iconic function of the expression. Had he given the sign's iconic function serious consideration, he would have resorted to an expression such as *blue blood* because the expression 'blue blood' is also used to refer to a person of aristocratic or wealthy ancestry.

On the other hand, some signs may have universal or nearly universal significance. Thus the colour 'red' signifies war or killings and related meanings in many cultures, but it also signifies prosperity in China and sex in Arabic. To illustrate, the following example taken from a short story titled مثوى *Dwelling* by Ḥaīfāʾ Zangana (cited in Almanna and Al-Rubaiʿi 2009: 52–53) may be considered:

يمازحها بائع الجرائد يسألها عن ليلتها. هل كانت ليلة حمراء؟ لا تقول شيئاً. تنظر إليه . . . لعدة ثوان ثم تسير.

A newspaper seller jokes with her about the previous night: Did she strike lucky? She doesn't reply, just staring at him for a while . . . and then off she goes.

As can be observed in the above example, a number of processes are employed by the writer:

a behavioural process	يمازحها بائع الجرائد •
a verbal process	يسألها عن ليلتها: هل كانت ليلة حمراء؟ •
a verbal process in the negative form	لا تقول شيئاً •
a behavioural process	تنظر إليه لعدة ثوان •
a material process	تسير. •

In يسألها عن ليلتها: هل كانت حمراء؟

- بائع الجرائد *the newspaper seller* used in the previous process is the Sayer/Asker,
- يسألها *to ask* is the process of saying,
- ها *her* is the addressee,
- عن ليلتها *about her night* is a matter circumstance, and
- هل كانت حمراء؟ which literally means *Was it red?* is the Verbiage of the process, that is to say, the content of what is said or indicated.

In this Verbiage of the process the 'red' colour is employed by the writer to talk about the addressee's night, thus implicitly referring to sexual issues. Taken into account that some colour terms may lose their colourness through translation, the translators have opted for a functional equivalent, thus preserving partially the sign's functions:

A newspaper seller jokes with her about the previous night: Did she strike lucky? She doesn't reply, just staring at him for a while . . . and then off she goes.

As such, writers, painters, designers and advertisers "try to choose colours that promote feelings of tranquillity" on the one hand, and "inspire to use such colours that affect people's feelings" (Sadkhan 2010: 73). Symbolic relationships are not restricted to colours but may apply to any element used in language (see the next section).

Symbols can be categorized into two types: local and universal. Mooij (1998: 45) argues that "symbols are words, gestures, pictures, or objects that carry a particular meaning recognized only by those who share a culture". It is the shared culture which determines whether a sign can be used as a symbol. People who share a particular culture may belong to different races, be from different countries, and may even speak different languages. In a globalized context, symbols which are restricted to particular cultures will not work for those who do not belong to the culture in which these symbols originated. Mooij further suggests that "symbols from one cultural group are regularly copied by others" (1998: 45). Copying a symbol implies a process in which this symbol is shown regularly through different media (including advertising) to a new audience, who consequently get used to perceiving the meaning of such a symbol. For example, the traditional dress of Arab men, which is a long, white garment with a shawl covering the head, is a sign symbolizing Arabs. This sign started to function as a symbol of Arabs through repetitive use by actors playing Arabs in Western films and wearing this dress. These actors need not speak a word of Arabic nor be of Arab origin themselves. The dress style is used only as a sign of Arab culture, even though many Arabs do not presently wear this kind of dress.

Another example which moved from being a local symbol to functioning globally in the same way is the crescent. This started out as a sign of Islam only among Muslims. Today, the crescent functions globally as a sign of Islam.

Now, let us consider the following advertisement that appeared in the magazine *19* (November 1999: 117) which attractively uses a symbolic relationship to stress the main feature of the advertised product. It starts with the heading *Some little luxuries last longer than others*, followed by a strawberry placed above a picture of the advertised product, Dove body wash. The first thing to attract the reader's attention is the combination of a strawberry and a body wash in the same advertisement, a combination which does not exist in nature. One is an item of food, and the other is used in the bath! This creates a kind of puzzle in the mind of the reader. The puzzle has to be solved, and this can only be achieved by reading the surrounding text. The heading stresses the feature of luxury, which is attributed to the advertised product. Traditionally, strawberries are a rather special fruit in the UK: somewhat expensive, seasonal and served on special occasions, and usually with cream, another item of luxury. With this in mind, it is not surprising to find that Arabs who originally belonged to another society and speak another language but who live in the UK can understand the symbolic link between luxury and strawberries. On the other hand, British people who live in a country where strawberries happen to be cheap will not necessarily interpret the strawberry in this advertisement as a symbol of luxury. Whether they do or not will depend on where they think the advertisement originated and their assumptions about the cultural background of the advertiser and intended audience. Thus the strawberry functions as a symbol of luxury only for UK residents and those who share the same practices.

Taking into account the symbolic function and its effect on people, the strawberry is replaced in another version of the advertisement (in *Newwoman*,

November 1999: 140) by three pieces of expensive chocolate, an item also traditionally associated with luxury. This is because a strawberry cannot have the same function in countries where strawberries are cheap and readily available.

Arab advertisers seem to manipulate iconic and indexical rather than symbolic relationships. One of the reasons for this preference for manipulating iconic and indexical relationships may be the nature of symbolic relationships, which require a deep understanding of culture and myths by the reader and more professional and manipulative skills by the advertiser. In addition, Arab advertisers often falsely assume that their Arab audience does not easily understand symbolic relationships. They rarely test their advertisements through questionnaires, surveys or by studying the influence of launching an advertising campaign on the sales income of the manufacturer. They often design an advertisement for long-term use, as if its impact is guaranteed forever. By testing the impact of their advertising methods, advertisers would be able to measure precisely the reaction of the consumers to particular concepts. Further, unlike English advertising, which frequently employs both local and universal symbols, Arabic advertising tends to rely more heavily on universal symbols. This seems to be the case in printed advertisements, but TV and radio advertisements tend to draw more heavily on local symbols.

Now, let us consider an advertisement for a type of Patek Philippe watch called Twenty~4.

The English version (quoted from Al-Shehari 2001: 189) pictures a female model called Bridget Hall wearing the advertised watch. In terms of iconicity, a relationship exists between the watch depicted on the left-hand side of the model and the watch worn by her. This relationship says: this watch is for wearing. Another iconic relationship operates between the brand of the watch, Twenty~4, which appears underneath the depicted product, and the number '24' in the slogan: Who will you be in the next 24 hours? This relationship consists of two types of iconic relationships: one is visual, occurring between the number '4' in the brand and the number '4' in the slogan, while another is phonological between 'Twenty' in the brand and the spoken first digit '2' of the number '24' in the slogan. The result is a part-visual, part-phonological iconic relationship between Twenty~4 and 24.

Who will you be in the next 24 hours?

In the Arabic version (Ibid.), the iconicity between the image of the watch on the left-hand side of the woman and the watch worn by her is maintained. The second relationship which occurs between Twenty~4 and the number '24' in the slogan is, however, lost. This is due to the process of translating the English slogan which contains the number 24 into Arabic as ٢٤, although the translator could have kept the English number, which originally comes from Arabic, in the Arabic text. The iconic relationships in the English version help to support a potential range of promotional messages intended by the advertiser, one of which might be something like: when you wear this watch, you will be as pretty and sexy as this model in just 24 hours. The focus here is the period of 24 hours, reminding us of the function of the watch but also indicating the time it takes to change into another person, perhaps a more glamorous one. It is clear that these relationships do not work in the same way in the Arabic version. However, Arab women who wear this type of watch are probably expected to be educated enough to be able to read the English brand name and to know its meaning and therefore to relate it to the corresponding sign 24.

من ستكونين في الـ ٢٤ ساعة المقبلة؟

The setting chosen for the English advertisement triggers particular connotations which are different from those produced in the Arabic text. In the English version, the model is wearing a black evening dress; she looks sexy and somewhat restless. She seems to be getting ready to go out to have fun and enjoy an evening of adventure. The time depicted is clearly evening. This meaning is supported by the dark background to the whole advertisement. In the Arabic version, the setting is different. The model is dressed casually and is sitting on a sofa. Judging by her relaxed posture, she seems to be in her own home. She is also wearing the advertised product on her left hand. The bright background subtly connotes a homely and social context. It suggests quiet happiness rather than the kind of fun associated with adventure: the happiness of homely comfort. Ideological viewpoints play an important part in this context and explain why such a sexy setting is chosen for the English advertisement, while a homely setting is chosen for the Arabic version. The difference here comes from the belief that young Arab women either should or do have as their priority getting married and having families, while the priority of European women of the same age is having fun. Thus, a different interpretation of the slogan is achieved in the Arabic version. The slogan in the English version, "Who will you be in the next 24 hours?" reminds the female consumer that she will be another person in 24 hours from the time of wearing this watch; she will be as pretty as the depicted model and will have more fun. Or it may suggest to the English-speaking consumer that the watch is a symbol of her freedom to be whoever she wants to be, whenever it suits her. On the other hand, the Arabic translation:

من ستكونين في الـ ٢٤ ساعة المقبلة؟

may suggest to the Arab woman that in 24 hours from the time of wearing this watch, she will be a different person; she will be as pretty as the depicted model and will get married and have a happy family. Alternatively, and this flexibility of interpretation is a feature of most successful advertising, it may communicate to the Arab woman a feeling of stability: you will always know who you are, safe and comfortable in your own surroundings.

In the previous example, the Arabic version of the advertisement succeeded in producing equivalent messages and impact as those intended by the English version. However, inappropriate manipulation of signs can sometimes cause loss of intended messages and impact. Advertisers tend to include a famous female or male personality in the promotional campaign in order to persuade the target readers, who are assumed to admire him/her, to buy a product or sign up for a service. Omega, for instance, chose a well-known female model, Cindy Crawford, to be pictured in all their campaigns for a new make of their watches called My Choice. For the purpose of illustration, let us take a more in-depth analysis of their English advertisement (published in *Marie Claire*, September 1999: 82) and its Arabic translation (published in *Sayidaty*, 23–29 January 1999: 5). The key element in both versions is the picture of Cindy Crawford wearing an Omega watch on her right wrist. This picture iconically represents the famous model Cindy Crawford. Inclusion of such a famous personality helps to associate the advertised product with positive features. According to Omega's International Marketing Director, Venanzio Ciampa:

> When we began designing the My Choice watch, which needed to embody elegance, beauty, style, sophistication and excellence, we knew we wanted input from a woman who exudes these same values and qualities. For us, the only woman to do this is Cindy Crawford . . . a true, modern Renaissance woman.

British readers of this advertisement, who know a great deal about Cindy Crawford and her private life, are more likely to attribute the features of Cindy Crawford, mentioned above by Venanzio Ciampa, to the product. The Arabic translation of this advertisement uses the same model, Cindy Crawford, to associate these features with the product. But do all or most Arab women know Cindy Crawford? Inclusion of such a model assumes that the readers know about her and will thus be able to combine such positive features with buying such a product. If the recipients of the Arabic text are not familiar with Cindy Crawford and her life, they are unlikely to be able to associate these features with the product. Replacing Cindy Crawford with another Arab star with similar features may, however, be a successful technique in this case.

The slogan at the top of the English advertisement says: Cindy Crawford's Choice. Under her picture, in her own hand, Cindy Crawford writes: Omega — my choice; the signature of Cindy Crawford concludes the handwritten slogan. The signature at the bottom bears an indexical relationship with Cindy Crawford in the sense that the signature is a physical feature of Crawford's personality. The signature here plays a role in certifying the statement at the top: Cindy Crawford's Choice. In the Arabic advertisement, the bottom line (Crawford's hand-writing and signature) is kept in English while the top line is translated literally into Arabic as:

اختيار سيندي كروفورد

Here, the indexical relationship remains, but it has no relation to the Arabic translation at the top unless Arab readers can understand the meaning of the handwritten slogan and the signature of Cindy Crawford, both of which appear in English.

Intertextuality

Julia Kristeva was the first to introduce the semiotic notion of 'intertextuality'. She defines intertextuality as the "transposition of one (or several) sign system(s) into another... [which] demands a new articulation of the thetic – of enunciative and denotative positionality" (1984: 59–60; quoted from a translation of her original work (1974) titled *La revolution du langage poétique*). A reference to a popular film may be included in an advertisement, hence two different systems are transposed. Each system of signs (plain text, film, advertisement, magazine article) exists in relation to other systems of signs. In fact, advertisements owe more to other advertisements, articles and references than to their producers in terms of interpretation. Kristeva's definition is particularly suitable for the context of advertising since a "system of signs" does not restrict intertextuality to texts. In our context, an advertisement (or any of its elements such as an image) may have a relationship with another advertisement, an article, a film, a popular place or a famous person. It is worth noting, however, that some definitions restrict intertextual relations to those existing between texts. Michael Riffaterre, for example, defines intertextuality as the reader's perception of the relations between a text and all the other texts that have preceded or followed it (Stam et al. 1992: 204). By way of explanation, the following example quoted from Choukri's novel الخبز الحافي (2000: 191; 6th edition) and translated by Bowles into *For Bread Alone* (1993: 143) may be given adequate consideration:

- إرادة الحياة، هذا هو معنى ما يقوله.
- وما معنى إرادة الحياة؟

48 A sign's functions and intertextuality

- إرادة الحياة معناها هو أنه إذا كان هناك شعب مستعبد أو إنسان ما وأراد أن يتحرر فإن الله له، والفجر يستجيب والقيد يستجيب يتهرس بقوة إرادة الحياة. *(p. 191)*

> He's talking about the desire to live.
> And what does the desire to live mean?
> "It means that if a man or a country is enslaved and decides to try and get free, Allah will help. He says: the dawn will respond and the chains will break because men will make it happen." (p. 143)

The writer, in creating his own text, opts for establishing an intertextual relation with two lines of poetry taken from a well-known poem entitled إرادة الحياة lit. *The Will of Life* written by the Tunisian poet 'Abū Al-Qāsim Al-Shābbī. By doing so, he transfers a set of micro signs that constitutes those two lines of poetry to his text, thus creating a mixture of signs (the signs of his own text and those signs referred to). Such a relationship created between the two sets of signs creates what is called by Peirce an 'interpretant' that works as an additional sign, thereby injecting the new text with a breath of allusion. Allusions can be brought from historical events, religious books, famous tales, poetry, etc. They are normally used to recall the qualities of the alluded. In this regard, Hatim and Mason (1990: 129) hold that:

> [E]ach intrusion of a citation in the text is the culmination of a process in which a sign travels from one text (source) to another (destination). The area being traversed from text to text is what we shall call the intertextual space.

Approached from a translation perspective, unlike other types of intertextuality in which famous people or places are alluded to, this type of intertextuality is hardly reflected in the TT. However, another intertextual relation between the original set of signs and the set of the translated signs is created because if there is no relationship or the relationship is very weak, then we cannot call it a translation – it might be re-writing or something else, depending on the strength of the relationship between the two sets of signs (for more details, see Almanna 2014).

To show how writers sometimes establish an intertextual relation with Quranic verses, let us consider the following example quoted from Mahfouz's novel (1977: 23) بداية ونهاية *The Beginning and the End* translated by Ramsis Awad (1985: 48):

target text	source text
Sometimes it is sinful to doubt.	معذرة يا بني إن بعض الظن إثم

> يا أيها الذين آمنوا اجتنبوا كثيرا من الظن إن بعض الظن إثم (سورة الحجرات، 12)
> O ye who believe! Avoid suspicion as much (as possible): for suspicion in some cases is a sin.

A sign's functions and intertextuality   49

Here, in an attempt to inject his text with vividness and make it more influential and persuasive, the original writer opts for building an intertextual relation with a Quranic آية *Ayaa* taken from سورة الحجرات Sūrat Al-Ḥujrāt, thereby transferring a set of religious signs to his text. Again, this type of intertextuality is not reflected in the TT. However, had the translator given full consideration to the intertextual relation between the source text and the Quranic verse, he could have opted for a rendering such as: *Excuse me my son, suspicion in some cases is a sin*, thus minimizing the degree of loss in terms of intertextuality as words like *suspicion* and *sin* are more formal and more likely to appear in a religious text.

To elaborate, the following painting by Laṭīf as-Samḥān can be considered. Although there is only one signifying system here, i.e. the pictorial system, the painter succeeds in injecting his painting with vividness, thus making it more influential.

Here, the painter, in an attempt to transfer a set of religious signs to his painting, tries to establish an intertextual relation with سورة يوسف Sūrat Yūsuf.

إن كان قميصه قدَّ من دبر فكذَّبت و هو من الصادقين (سورة يويف، أية 27)

As can be seen, the shirt in the painting is torn by the effect of some bullets from the back, not from the front, therefore, this shirt can be used as a symbol for all truthful people. As the shirt is without a body, this evokes in our mind the Prophet Yusuf's story and his 11 brothers who were jealous from him to the degree that they started plotting about how to dispose him. One day, hardly had they been far enough from home and came across a dry well when they removed his shirt and threw their younger brother in the well, irrespective of his pleas. They left him there to die of hunger. On their way back home, they slaughtered a goat and stained his shirt with its blood.

They told their father their younger brother was eaten by a wolf while they were grazing their sheep. We, as viewers, can invoke the whole story thanks to the shirt along with the drops of blood. This fits hand in glove with Kristeva (1984), who refuses to accept the naive notion of a textual understanding between a sender and a receiver suggested by a simplified model of communication (Nöth 1990: 322). Instead of studying the text as a communicative process of social exchange, Kristeva (Ibid.) approaches the text as 'signifying practices' which refer to differentiated signifying systems. Every sign in an advertisement or painting infuses it with a particular system of signifying practices. A film hero in an advertisement, for example, brings to mind all the practices which are associated with the hero: physical features, style of life, way of speaking, etc. A picture of a well-known place brings different systems of signs into the mind, such as location, weather, history, politics, etc.

By way of illustration, let us consider an advertisement for Nescafé, produced by Nestlé UK Ltd. in York.

The advertisement features a picture of Chris Eubank, a famous English boxer, holding the Nescafé cup in his hand. Next to his picture there appears the slogan *Thimply the betht.* which seems to be uttered by Eubank himself. There are two signifying systems here: pictorial and verbal. The pictorial system relates to the picture of Chris Eubank. Chris Eubank is known to have a lisp and to speak with a soft tone.

His voice is quietly feminine. People like doing impressions of him, i.e. copying his way of speaking. All these features are practices which signify for consumers a well-known personality, a personality with whom they might want to identify: the smart hero with a sense of humour. The verbal element, the slogan, also encodes a practice signifying Eubank: this is realized through a typographical representation of his lisp. Typing this slogan as if it is spoken with a lisp indexically indicates its speaker. In addition, the slogan in this form indicates Eubank's soft and feminine manner of speech.

The manipulation of Eubank's picture in the advertisement is one example of intertextuality, known as 'intertextual reference'. Here, the reference is to a person, a place, an event, a film, etc. For Kristeva, the text is an insertion of texts and codes, i.e. "the absorption and transformation of another text" (1980: 37, in Nöth 1990: 323). The insertion of an intertextual reference aims at creating new meanings to be associated with the advertised product other than those direct or denotative meanings with which we may normally associate it. Bignell (1997) explains how these new meanings of the advertisement are only perceived when the cultural knowledge which is presumed to exist for the reader is used to decode the intertextual reference in the advertisement. He adds: "Many of the signs in the ad function as clues to help us select the appropriate cultural knowledge, and to eliminate knowledge which is not appropriate" (p. 44). For instance, it does not matter, in the advertisement discussed above, whether we know when and where Eubank had been boxing and with whom. It does not matter whether we know his personal details, such as where he lives, who his wife is and how many children he has. On the other hand, it is important to know the attributes of publicity, victory, humour and glamour which are associated with Chris Eubank; it is these attributes which are meant to be associated with the advertised product.

Intertextual links cross the boundaries of different genres and systems of signs. Genres can be identified on the basis of shared functions. Advertising, for instance, is a genre that aims at selling a product or a service. However, a film is a genre that consists of a series of actions to be watched by an audience for the purpose of entertainment, and news is a genre that provides the audience with reports about particular events. Each genre may in turn consist of different types communicated through different media. Each type of sub-genre shares conventions with other members of the genre. For example, the genre of advertising represents different types such as printed advertising and audio/visual advertising. Printed advertisements can be published in magazines, in newspapers or as posters. Audio/visual advertising, on the other hand, can be seen on television, cinemas and on the Internet or heard on radio. To explain, Nescafé Original has always been Britain's favourite cup of coffee (so claim the advertisers!), drunk by more people, from all walks of life, than any other coffee. The latest advertising campaign of Nescafé, on TV, posters and radio, shows that Britain's best-loved celebrities think the same about Nescafé Original as everyone else – it is the best coffee you can drink. TV commercials feature Denise van Outen and Ian Wright. Both, as well as Chris Eubank, appear on a series of posters. Being 'the best' is the main feature promoted for Nescafé. This confirmation of Nescafé's superiority is delivered to consumers from the mouths of their best-loved heroes and repeated in a variety of posters and printed advertisements. Denise van Outen is featured in a road poster holding the distinctive cup of Nescafé and saying:

> *the original and still the best*

The best here reminds the reader of the *betht* in Eubank's poster. Thus, intertextual relationships play an important role in emphasizing selling points.

One commercial that demonstrates intertextuality among advertisements for the same product published in different media, namely print and television, was featured on Channel 4 and other channels in the UK in the winter of 1999. An intertextual relationship exists between the printed advertisement about Nescafé – and other printed advertisements of Nescafé – and the televised commercials about Nescafé. One commercial features Denis van Outen, who used to present the TV series *The Big Breakfast*. *The Big Breakfast* is the UK's breakfast TV show on Channel 4 which provides the audience with a mixture of interviews, news, quiz games and features. The advertisement started with Outen wearing expensive clothes and shoes, walking in a street full of poor terraced houses, then one of her heels is broken. An old woman, who seems to be poor, is shown standing in front of her house when Outen's heel breaks. She immediately says to Outen: *I have some glue inside. Are you sure?* Outen replies. The scene moves inside the old woman's house, where we see Outen drinking from the Nescafé red cup, and then saying *Nice One. Quality pays, remember that when you buy cheap shoes*, the old woman says. Outen shrugs her shoulders and smiles. The scene moves outside the house with the old woman saying bye to Outen and a young boy, who seems to be a relative of the old woman, appearing and looking surprised at seeing van Outen there. The old woman says to the boy: *I know what you think, cheap shoes.*

Another television commercial about Nescafé makes use of an intertextual reference to the famous footballer Ian Wright, who used to play for the English Arsenal Club. It is raining; the setting is a wealthy residential area with beautiful gardens. Ian Wright emerges from a posh black sports car which has just broken down, runs in the rain and knocks on someone's door. A white man opens the door. He is astonished to see Ian Wright and says: *Ian Wright!*. Then Wright asks him if he could use his telephone. The scene then moves into the sitting room to show Ian Wright raising the Nescafé cup and saying: *Nice One*. The man's wife comes in and asks her husband if he has someone with him; he immediately replies in astonishment: *Ian Wright!*. The camera moves outside the house where Ian Wright thanks the man and walks until he reaches the gate of the garden, then the man raises the Nescafé cup and says loudly, as if shouting in a football match: *Ian Wright Wright Wright*. Ian Wright is amused and leaves.

As the manufacturer of Nescafé emphasizes that the product is liked by all different classes and groups of people, the promotion campaign tends to include intertextual references to stars of different racial backgrounds and social groups. Chris Eubank and Ian Wright are black and male while Denise Outen is white and female. Filming these stars, who are supposed to be wealthy, in poor areas and meeting poor people makes the distance between classes seem trivial where Nescafé is concerned. It suggests that Nescafé is loved by all classes and groups of people. This variety of background and lack of social barriers are communicated to the viewer by means of intertextual links, connecting the printed advertisement of Chris Eubank with the TV commercials of Ian Wright and Denis Outen.

Fiske argues that "the meanings generated by any one text are determined partly by the meanings of other texts to which it appears similar" (1990: 166). This applies to relationships between an advertisement and another one which promotes the same product and is similar in terms of form, medium of publishing and intended messages. An example of this type of relationship can be seen in the three advertisements promoting Nescafé in different magazines at the same time (cited in Al-Shehari 2001: 149).

A sign's functions and intertextuality 53

They are all printed against a red background, with the same format of a picture of a person with a caption on a white background under each one, each with the Nescafé logo in the top left corner. Further, these advertisements were all placed on the back covers of the magazines concerned. All these technical features make it easier for the viewer to establish the required links between the advertisements.

As can be seen, one of the advertisements shows a beautiful lady in a smart coat – she appears to be coming back home after spending the evening out. It looks as if the lady was accompanied by her (boy)friend, who is not visible in the picture. This assumption is supported by the caption under the picture which says:

> *Sorry you can't come in for one!*

It would be normal for the lady to invite her boyfriend for a cup of coffee, in this case Nescafé. A woman inviting her boyfriend in for a cup of coffee in British culture also suggests a sexual motivation. The word *one* in this caption carries two meanings: denotative and connotative. The former is *one cup of Nescafé* while the other is *one sexual visit*. The reader of this advertisement is offered two different meanings. These meanings go through a process of filtration whereby the intended meaning becomes more dominant. This is achieved through intertextual links that occur with the distinctive use of the word *one* in other advertisements of Nescafé.

54 A sign's functions and intertextuality

By contrast, another advertisement shows a woman in casual clothes at home calling someone on the phone and saying:

> *Why don't you come over for one?*

The context here suggests that the woman is inviting a friend to come for a cup of Nescafé.

Another advertisement shows a young man who is about to get up but is still in bed saying:

> *can't start the day without one*

Again, the denotative meaning of *one* is very clear in this advertisement as *one cup of Nescafé*. A new connotative meaning communicated here is that Nescafé gives you energy to start the day. It should be clear now how intertextuality among these advertisements helps in emphasizing the link between sex, socializing and energy in relation to the advertised product.

Arabic advertising does not seem to employ intertextual links, including intertextual references, extensively. Having consulted a huge number of advertisements, we can readily conclude that very few Arabic advertisements refer to other advertisements or contain references to famous Arab personalities. When they do, it tends to be in the context of promoting only imported products so that the feature of 'intertextuality' cannot function effectively in many cases. The advertisements are occasionally translated or localized by means of replacing the original personalities with Arab ones, but this strategy of substitution is not very common.

To make this point clear, let us discuss one of the Arabic advertisements about Lux soap. Here, an Egyptian actress is used to persuade consumers to buy the product. Further, the advertisement starts with information to the reader about the same actress appearing on TV to recommend the product. Here, the advertiser attempts to establish a direct intertextual link to another advertisement about the product, which had been featured in a different medium. Intertextual reference in English advertising tends to be established in more subtle and more playful ways, without spelling out the link for the consumer.

Key technical terms

- Connotation
- Denotation
- Iconic function
- Indexical function
- Interpretant
- Interpretive semiotics
- Intertextuality
- Symbolic function

Exercises

Exercise 1: Translate the following sentences into Arabic, paying extra attention to the colour terms (highlighted for you), then discuss whether these colour terms have lost their colourness through translation or not.

My youngest sister was the **black sheep** in our family; she dropped out of school at the age of 18.
The thief was caught **red-handed** stealing some cosmetics.
You know him very well: he always has **the blues** during the exam time.
As I am extremely busy, we go out for dinner **once in a blue moon**.
– Why did you tell your mom that the cake was delicious?
– It is just **a white lie**.
You can tell by his garden that he **has a green thumb**.
You have to know that I was not **born with a silver spoon in my mouth**.
The conference was **a golden opportunity** for me to meet up with some scholars and researchers.
Barely had the soldiers seen the enemy when they **raised a white flag** and surrendered.
We have got **the green light** from the dean to organize the party.
She argued with her manager until she was **blue in the face**.
Once the teacher asked me, I became **red in the face**.

Exercise 2: In the following painting by Laṭīf as-Samḥān discussed in this chapter, had the painter, for example, changed the direction of the shirt to indicate that it is torn by the effect of the bullets that enter the shirt from the front, would he have failed to establish an intertextual relation with سورة يوسف Sūrat Yūsuf? Discuss.

Exercise 3: The following example is quoted from Mahfouz's (1961/1973: 40) novel اللص والكلاب *The Thief and the Dogs* and translated by Adel Ata Elyas

(1987: 118). Comment on any sign that needs special treatment and how it has been translated.

He felt a magic scent in the air, something he couldn't identify in spite of his long sharp nose. It was the smell of aristocracy.	وثمة رائحة سحرية لا تصدر إلا من دم أزرق رغم أنفه المائل إلى الفطس.

Exercise 4: The following examples are quoted from different bilingual sources. Comment on the colour terms used in the original texts along with their translations. Have they lost their colourness when being translated from Arabic to English?

As soon as I set eyes upon him, I realised the reason why my wife had blown our meagre savings, which I was putting aside for a rainy day, on such ridiculous attire. (Almanna and Al-Rubai'i 2009: 74–75)	وما أن انتقلت عيناي إليه حتى علمت لماذا نسفت زوجتي مدخراتنا المتواضعة لليوم الأسود لتبددها على الزي القرقوزي المضحك...
The director was sporting such loud colours: a fiery, bright red shirt, loud, buttercup yellow trousers and a tie wider than the palm of my hand, festooned with all the colours of the springtime flowers in Hawaii. What was even more absurd was his pair of violet socks. (Ibid.)	...فالمدير يرتدي الألوان الصارخة نفسها: قميص أحمر ناري وهاج، سروال أصفر فاقع بلون الورس الصافي، رباط أعرض من كفي ازدهرت عليه كل ورود هاواي في الربيع، والأغرب من كل ذلك جوربان بنفسجيان...
So he began to increase the frequency of his walks outside, in squares and public gardens. He would look at the sea, addicted to thinking about this girl who had suddenly entered his life just as she had entered his classroom, out of the blue. (Husni and Newman 2008: 94–95)	...فصار يكثر الذهاب إلى الخلاء، والميادين الرحبة الفسيحة، والحدائق العامة، وتأمل البحر وإدمان التفكير في هذه البنت التي دخلت فجأة حياته كما دخلت فجأة حجرة الدرس.
Aziza was a beautiful girl with a fear of black cats. She looked worried the moment she sat down in front of Sheikh Said. His eyes were jet-black and fiery. (Ibid.: 44–45)	عزيزة صبية جميلة، تخاف القطط السوداء، ولقد كانت مضطربة لحظة قعدت قبالة الشيخ سعيد، وكانت عيناه قطعتين من السواد المتوحش.
The neon lights came on inside the restaurant, their bluish white light absorbing the faces and hands of those who were seated. In their seats they were tired, with yellow faces, as if they were suffering from a lack of sleep. (Sadkhan and Pragnell 2012: 32–33)	اضيئت مصابيح النيون داخل المطعم، ضوؤها الأبيض المزرق يمتص وجوه الجالسين وأيديهم. كانوا، وهم في مقاعدهم، مرهقين، صفر الوجوه، وكأنهم يشكون نقصا من النوم.

While I was in bed this morning, I caught a glimpse of the movement of clouds: mountains of cotton and birds, like white threads, with trimmed wings; swirls of foam inflated in a milk-coloured sky; and a piece of the sun running gleefully among the clouds, appearing and disappearing, creeping among the trees, the buildings and the sides of the minaret.
(Ibid.: 92–93)

هذا الصباح لمحت وأنا في فراشي حركة تنقّل الغيوم: تلال قطنية وطيور، مثل خيوط بيض، مقصوصة الأجنحة وسورات من رغوة منفوشة في سماء بلون الحليب وكسرة من قرص الشمس تركض جذلة بين السحب، تظهر وتختفي، متسللة من بين الأشجار والمباني وحواف المئذنة.

Further reading

Almanna, A. (2016a). *The Routledge Course in Translation Annotation: Arabic-English-Arabic*. London/New York: Routledge.
———. (2016b). *Semantics for Translation Students: Arabic-English-Arabic*. Oxford: Peter Lang.
Al-Rubai'i, A. (2005). *Translation Criticism*. Durham: Durham Modern Languages Series.
Al-Shehari, K. (2001). *The Semiotics and Translation Advertising Texts: Conventions, Constraints and Translation Strategies with Particular Reference to English and Arabic*, unpublished Ph.D. thesis: University of Manchester.
Faiq, S. and Sabry, R. (2013). "Altered Semiotics Through Translation", *Sayyab Translation Journal*, Vol. 5, pp. 45–56.
Grutman, R. (2009). "Multilingualism". In M. Baker and G. Saldanha (eds.), *Routledge Encyclopedia of Translation Studies* (2nd edn), pp. 182–185. London/New York: Routledge.
Gully, A. (1996–1997). "The Discourse of Arabic Advertising: Preliminary Investigations", *Journal of Arabic and Islamic Studies*, Vol. 1, pp. 1–49.
Hatim, B. and Mason, I. (1990). *Discourse and the Translator*. London: Longman.
Pertilli, S. (1992). "Translation, Semiotics and Ideology", *TTR: Traduction, Terminologie, Redaction*, Vol. 5 (1), pp. 233–264.
Vestergaard, T. and Schroder, K. (1985). *The Language of Advertising*. Oxford: Basil Blackwell.

References

Adab, B. J. (1997). *Translation Strategies and Cross-Cultural Constraints: A Case Study of the Translation of Advertising Texts*, unpublished Ph.D. thesis: Aston University.
Almanna, A. (2014). *Translation Theories Exemplified from Cicero to Pierre Bourdieu*. München: Lincom Europa Academic Publishers.
———. (2016a). *The Routledge Course in Translation Annotation: Arabic-English-Arabic*. London/New York: Routledge.
———. (2016b). *Semantics for Translation Students: Arabic-English-Arabic*. Oxford: Peter Lang.
Almanna, A. and Al-Rubai'i, A. (2009; bilingual edn). *Modern Iraqi Short Stories: A Bilingual Reader*. London: Sayyab Books Ltd.
Al-Rubai'i, A. (2005). *Translation Criticism*. Durham: Durham Modern Languages Series.
Al-Shehari, K. (2001). *The Semiotics and Translation Advertising Texts: Conventions, Constraints and Translation Strategies with Particular Reference to English and Arabic*, unpublished Ph.D. thesis: University of Manchester.
Awad, R. (trans.) (1985). *The Beginning and the End*. Cairo: American University in Cairo Press.
Bignell, J. (1997). *Media Semiotics*. Manchester: Manchester University Press.
Bowles, P. (trans.) (1993). *For Bread Alone*. London: Saqi Books.
Choukri, M. الخبز الحافي (2000). (6th edn). London: Saqi Books.

de Saussure, F. (1916/83). *Cours de Linguistique Générale*, Paris: Editions Payot, translated by R. Harris as *Course in General Linguistics*. London: Duckworth.

Elyas, A. E. (trans.) (1987). *The Thief and the Dogs*. Jeddah: Dār Al-Shurūq.

Faiq, S. and Sabry, R. (2013). "Altered Semiotics Through Translation", *Sayyab Translation Journal*, Vol. 5, pp. 45–56.

Farghal, M. (2012). *Advanced Issues in Arabic-English Translation Studies*. Kuwait: Kuwait University Press.

Farghal, M. and Almanna, A. (2015). *Contextualizing Translation Theories: Aspects of Arabic – English Interlingual Communication*. Newcastle upon Tyne, England: Cambridge Scholars Publishing.

Fiske, J. (1990). *Introduction to Communication Studies*. London: Routledge.

Grutman, R. (2009). "Multilingualism". In M. Baker and G. Saldanha (eds.), *Routledge Encyclopedia of Translation Studies* (2nd edn), pp. 182–185. London/New York: Routledge.

Gully, A. (1996–1997). "The Discourse of Arabic Advertising: Preliminary Investigations", *Journal of Arabic and Islamic Studies*, Vol. 1, pp. 1–49.

Halliday, M. A. K. (1976). "Notes on Transitivity and Theme in English: Part 2", *Journal of Linguistics*, Vol. 3 (1), pp. 199–244.

Jakobson, R. (1959/1992). "On Linguistic Aspects of Translation". In R. Schulte and J. Biguenet (eds.), *Theories of Translation: An Anthology of Essays from Dryden to Derrida*, pp. 144–151. Chicago/London: University of Chicago Press.

Hatim, B. and Mason, I. (1990). *Discourse and the Translator*. London: Longman.

Hodge, R. and Kress, G. (1988). *Social Semiotics*. Cambridge: Polity Press.

Kristeva, J. (1984). *Revolution in Poetic Language*, trans. by M. Waller (1974) from *La rivolution du langage poitique*. New York: Columbia University Press.

Lemke, J. L. (1987). "Social Semiotics and Science Education", *The American Journal of Semiotics*, Vol. 5 (2), pp. 217–232.

Liardet, F. (trans.) (1993). *Adrift on the Nile: Nobel Laureates in Search of Identity and Integrity: Voices of Different Cultures*. New York: Doubleday.

Mahfouz, N. (1961/1973). اللص والكلاب. Cairo: Maktabat Miṣr.

———. (1966). ثرثرة فوق النيل. Cairo: Dār Miṣr liltibāʻa.

———. (1971/1977). بداية ونهاية. Beirut: Dār Al-Qalam.

Mooij, M. K. de (1998). *Global Marketing and Advertising: Understanding Cultural Paradoxes*. Los Anglos/London/New Delhi: Sage Publications.

Nöth, W. (1990). *Handbook of Semiotics*. Bloomington: Indiana University Press.

Oxford Word Power Dictionary for Learners of English. (2006). Oxford: Oxford University Press.

Peirce, C. S. (1931–1958). *Collected Papers*. Volumes 1–6: Hartshorne, C. and Weiss, P. (eds.), Volumes 7–8: Burks, A. W. (ed.), Cambridge, MA: Belknap Press, Harvard University Press. (In-text references are to CP, followed by volume and paragraph numbers).

Pertilli, S. (1992). "Translation, Semiotics and Ideology", *TTR: Traduction, Terminologie, Redaction*, Vol. 5 (1), pp. 233–264.

Sadkhan, R. (2010). "Translation of Colour Metaphor: A Collocational and Idiomatic Perspective". In S. Faiq and A. Clark (eds.), *Beyond Denotation in Arabic-English Translation*, pp. 72–91. London: Sayyab Books Ltd.

Sadkhan, R. and Pragnell, F. (2012). رائحة الشتاء *The Scent of Winter: A Bilingual Reader*. London: Sayyab Books Ltd.

Stam, R., Burgoyne, R. and Flitterman-Lewis, S. (1992). *New Vocabularies in Film Semiotics: Structuralism, Post-Structuralism and Beyond*. London: Routledge.

Vestergaard, T. and Schroder, K. (1985). *The Language of Advertising*. Oxford: Basil Blackwell.

4
TRANSITIVITY SYSTEM

In this chapter, transitivity processes according to Halliday's Systemic Functional Grammar – as to whether they represent an event, action, saying, behaviour, state of mind, state of being or state of existing – are presented and seen through the prism of translation. These processes (be they material, verbal, behavioural, mental, relational or existential) are studied in this chapter as parameters to test translation accuracy. It is hypothesized here that in order to create a similar mental image in the target-language readers' minds, the translators need to give these processes along with their participants and circumstances full consideration. What will happen to the mental image if the process is changed, the circumstance becomes a process or the other way around, a process is added or deleted, etc.? All these questions are addressed in this chapter.

Transitivity

Transitivity is defined by Halliday (1976: 199) from a functional point of view as "the set of options relating to cognitive content, the linguistic representation of extralinguistic experience, whether of the phenomena of the external world or of feelings, thoughts and perceptions". In the sense that Halliday uses the term, transitivity generally refers to the way in which meaning is encoded and presented in a clause. According to Halliday's (1994) Systemic Functional Grammar, the process of making meanings is simply a process of selecting certain elements from the linguistic system and excluding others as opting for other elements may well create different meanings, and so on (Halliday 1994: XIV). Our socio-cultural experience "consists of 'goings-on' – happening, doing, sensing, meaning, and being and becoming. All these goings-on are sorted out in the grammar of the clause" (Halliday 1994: 106). Cast in less technical terms, these socio-cultural experiences can be encoded and presented by language users in a clause, thus reflecting the mental image that they have of the world around them. This fits hand in glove with Simpson's (1993: 88) view that the transitivity model in discourse analysis shows how language users (be they speakers or writers) "encode in language their mental picture of reality and how they account for their experiences in the world around them". This view is adopted in the current study.

In transitivity, a number of processes can be identified as to whether they represent an event, action, saying, behaviour, state of mind, state of being or state of existing. With this in mind, these processes can be classified into a number of processes, such as a material process, a verbal process, a behavioural process, a mental process, a relational process and an existential process. In what follows, these processes are explained with reference to translation.

Material processes

In material processes (also known as processes of doing and happening), there is an obligatory role of Actor filled by the doer of the process, an optional role of Goal filled by the entity affected by the process, and an optional role of Recipient or Client that construes a benefactive role – "they represent a participant that is benefitting from the performance of the process, in terms of either goods or services. The Recipient is one that goods are given to; the Client is one that services are done for" (Halliday and Matthiessen [1985] 2014: 237). By way of explanation, the following sentence can be discussed:

قتلَ اللصُّ المرأة بالسِّكين.

Here, a material process is expressed where:

- اللصّ *the thief* is the Actor of the process, that is, the doer of the act of killing,
- المرأة *the woman* is the Goal of the process, that is, the affected participant, and
- السّكين *the knife* is the instrument used by the Actor to commit the act of killing.

It is worth noting that the Client of the process is backgrounded in attention in this example. Further, in this process, as there are no goods to be given to somebody; there is no Recipient.

To elaborate, the following two examples extracted from *BBC* (23 October 2017) are considered here:

> *Just last month, another of its journalists, Yulia Latynina, left the country after she was sprayed with faeces and her car was set on fire.*
> وغادرت يوليا لاتينينا، الصحفية التي تعمل في إيكو موسكوفي أيضا، البلاد الشهر الماضي عقب تعرضها للقذف بالفضلات وإحراق سيارتها.

As can be observed, three material processes are employed in this example. These are:

- *Yulia Latynina left the country*, where *Yulia Latynina* is the Actor of the material process. In this process, an open path with gapping over the medial and final portions of the path is utilized in both versions. While the starting point (her country) is foregrounded in attention, the endpoint (to somewhere) is backgrounded in attention.
- *she was sprayed with faeces*, where the pronoun *she* is the Goal of the process filling a semantic role of Affected Participant and the Actor is backgrounded in attention.
- *her car was set on fire*, where *her car* is the Affected Participant, and the Actor is backgrounded in attention.

It is worth noting that the act of leaving the country occurred after the act of her being sprayed with faeces and the act of setting fire to her car. By the effect of عقب *after*, a time lapse between the act of leaving the country and the other two acts is created by the news editor.

Following is the second example:

> *A male suspect is under arrest. His motive is not clear, though police say it appears to be a personal grudge.*
> ألقت الشرطة القبض على المشتبه به في تنفيذ الهجوم، لكن دوافعه لا تزال غير معروفة. غير أن الشرطة ترجح أن سبب الهجوم عداوة شخصية.

Here, in the first tensed clause, a material process is employed by *BBC* in its Arabic version where الشرطة *the police* is the Actor of the process, and المشتبه به *the suspect* is the Goal, that is, the Affected Participant. This material process is changed by *BBC* in its English version to a process of being, thus (1) shifting our focus of attention towards the state of the suspect after the act of arresting, which is backgrounded in attention and (2) creating a time lapse between the act of arresting him by the police and the suspect's being under arrest. Had the news editor or trans-editor opted for a different grammatical form and content specifications, such as *the police arrested the suspect* or *the suspect was arrested by the police*, s/he would have produced a similar mental image.

62 Transitivity system

To elaborate, these two *Reuters* news items on the same topic (one in English and the other in Arabic, 3 April 2015) may be considered:

On April 1, the city of Tikrit was liberated from the extremist group Islamic State.
في الأول من ابريل/نيسان جرى تحرير مدينة تكريت من تنظيم الدولة الإسلامية.

Here, a material process (*was liberated* = جرى تحرير) in the passive voice is employed by *Reuters* in its both versions where:

- *Iraqi forces* = القوات العراقية is the Actor of the process, but is backgrounded in attention, and
- *the city of Tikrit* = مدينة تكريت is the Goal of the process (when we focus on its infrastructure, etc.) and the Client of the process (when we focus on its people).

This material process evokes in our mind another material process, i.e. *the city of Tikrit was occupied by the extremist group of Islamic State* where:

- *the extremist group of Islamic State* is the Actor of the process who occupied the city some time ago, and
- *the city of Tikrit* is the Goal of the process, i.e. the Affected Participant.

The lexical item *liberate* indicates that the liberator, i.e. Iraq, is the land Possessor in a process of having, such as *Iraq owns the city of Tikrit* or *the city of Tikrit belongs to Iraq* (for more details, see the process of having below).

Mental processes

Unlike material processes, which are concerned with experiences of the material world, mental processes (also known as processes of sensing) represent conscious experiences as they flow from a person's consciousness – person here refers to all animates (Halliday and Matthiessen [1985] 2014: 245). Mental processes express a state of mind or psychological events; therefore, they have to do with feelings, thinking, perceiving and wanting, that is, they are internal reactions to different phenomena. Mental processes are classified by Halliday (1994: 116–118; also discussed in Halliday and Matthiessen [1985] 2014: 257; Mattthiessen 2004: 208–210) into four types, namely 'emotion', 'cognition', 'perception' and 'desideration'. Following are the common verbs that can serve as mental processes in both languages (Almanna 2018: 112–113):

1. *emotion*, expressed by verbs, such as: *to love, to fancy, to hate, to like, to dislike, to adore, to detest, to regret, to enjoy, to fear*, etc. أحبّ، إستهوى، عشق، أعجب بـ، مال إلى، هوى، ودّ، كرَهَ، مقتَ، بغضَ، نفرَ من، اشمأزَ من، أسِف، ندم، إستمتَعَ، تَمَتَّع، خاف (إنتابه) الخوف ...

2   *cognition*, expressed by verbs, such as: *to know, to understand, to comprehend, to remember, to believe, to realize, to recognize*, etc.

عَرِفَ، ألَمَ ب، بصرَ ب، علِمَ، اطَّلَعَ على، فَهِم، استَوعب، تذكَّر، اعتقَد، أدركَ، ميَّزَ، تعرَّف على، لحظ الفرق، تبيَّن، استشفَّ ...

3   *perception*, expressed by verbs, such as: *to see, to hear, to overhear, to feel, to notice, to perceive, to sense, to taste, to smell*, etc.

رأى، سمِعَ، شعرَ، لاحظَ، أحسَّ، حسَّ، أبصرَ، تذوَّق، شمَّ ...

4   *desideration*, expressed by verbs, such as: *to want, to desire, to intend, to hope for, to yearn for, to plan, to determine, to decide*, etc.

أراد، رغبَ، نوى، قصدَ، اعتزمَ، سعى، رمى إلى، أملَ، خطَّط، تاقَ إلى، تطلَّع إلى، جنِبَ إلى، صمَّم، عقد العزم على، قرَّر ...

In mental processes, there are two participants: one is an obligatory role of Senser filled by the entity that feels, thinks, or perceives, and the other is an optional role of Phenomenon filled by the entity that is felt, thought, or perceived by the Senser. To illustrate, the following example can be considered:

رأى الرَّجلُ فتاةً صغيرة تحمل ناظورًا.

Here, there is a mental process (perception) where:

- الرجل *the man* is the person who saw the young girl with the naked eye, thus indicating that the distance between them is not that great, and
- فتاة صغيرة *a little girl* is what is seen by the man.

It is worth noting that the clause تحمل ناظورًا *[she] holds a pair of binoculars* modifies the noun phrase فتاة صغيرة *a little girl* in the above example. With this in mind, this sentence can be translated as *The man saw a little girl holding a pair of binoculars*.

To reinforce this point, the following example extracted from a short story titled ليلة القهر *Night of Torment* by Layla Al-'Uthmān (translated by and cited in Husni and Newman 2008: 260–261) may be considered:

سمعته ينشق نشقات متتالية سريعة كمن يبحث عن مصدر رائحة ما! أدركت أنه اكتشف رائحة جديدة.

Here, three mental processes are employed by the author. They are:

- سمعته where the implicit pronoun هي *she* is the Senser, سمع *to hear* is the process of sensing,

- أدركت *she realized*, where the implicit pronoun هي *she* is the Senser and أدرك *to realize* is the process of sensing, and
- اكتشف *he discovered*, where the implicit pronoun هو *he* is the Senser and اكتشف *to discover* is the process of sensing.

These processes along with their participants and circumstances have been translated into (the processes and participants' roles are added):

... *she* [Senser] *heard* [process of sensing] *him sniffing – fast, repetitive sniffs – like someone trying to ascertain the source of a particular smell. She* [Senser] *realized* [process of sensing] *that he* [Senser] *had discovered* [process of sensing] *a new smell.*

Verbal processes

Verbal processes (also known as processes of saying) include all modes of expressing and indicating. They can be either explicit when verbs such as *to say, to tell, to utter, to inform, to express, to complain* and so on are used or implicit when verbs such as *to show, to indicate*, etc. are employed. Following are examples of the common verbs that can serve as verbal processes in both languages (Almanna 2018: 109–110):

| to say, to tell, to utter, to ask, to enquire, to command, to order, to require, to threaten, to beg, to implore, to add, to reply, to urge, to inform, to complain, to report, to announce, to notify, to explain, to suggest, to claim, to assert, to confirm, to argue, to persuade, to convince, to promise, to praise, to flatter, to congratulate, to insult, to slander, to abuse, to blame, to rebuke, to criticize, to chide, to accuse, to censure, etc. | قال، أخبر، تفوّه، سأل، استفسر، استعلم، أمر، هدّد، توسّل، استعطف، استجدى، تضرّع، ناشد، التمس، هتف، أضاف، أجاب، ألحّ، أبلغ، بلّغ، أعلم، اشتكى، أعلن، شرح، وضّح، اقترح، زعم، ادّعى، أكّد، جادل، ناقش، أقنع، وعد، مدحَ، جاملَ، هنأ، أهان، سبّ، شهّرَ، لام، ذمّ، وبّخ، قرّع، انتقد، أنّب، عنّف، زجرَ، اتّهمَ، أدان، ندّد، استنكر، استهجن، شجب ... |

In verbal processes, four roles filled by four participants can be realized: an obligatory role of Sayer filled by the addresser, an optional role of Receiver filled by the addressee, an optional role of Target filled by the entity targeted by the verbal process, and the role of Verbiage filled by the content of what is said or the name of the saying. To explain, the following example extracted from a short story titled الشباك والساحة *The Window and the Courtyard* by Maḥmūd 'Abdulwahhāb (translated by and cited in Sadkhan and Pragnell 2012: 10–11) may be considered:

قال [process of saying] أحد المارة [Sayer] وهو يرفع رأسه [circumstance]:
- إنهم فوقنا يشربون الشاي ويقرأون الصحف [Verbiage].

In this example, a verbal process is utilized by the writer where أحد المارة *one of the passers-by* is the Sayer, قال *said* is the process of saying in the past where the emphasis is placed on the completion of the act of saying, وهو يرفع رأسه *while raising his head* is a circumstantial element (manner/quality as it answers the question 'how') where there is no time interval between the act of saying and the act of raising his head, and إنهم فوقنا يشربون الشاي ويقرأون الصحف *they are above us drinking tea and reading newspapers*

Transitivity system 65

is the Verbiage of the process, that is, the content of what is said or indicated. However, the role of Receiver, that is, the addressee, is not expressed explicitly by the writer in an attempt to get his readers physically involved in the text interpretation (for more details on this example, see next chapter). This has been translated as (processes and participants' roles are added):

> "*Above us they are drinking tea and reading newspapers*" [Verbiage]*, said* [process of saying] *a passer-by* [Sayer] *raising his head.*

To reinforce this point, the following example adapted from Hans Küng's Book *Islam: Past, Present and Future* (translated by and cited in Al-Shuraīqī 2016: 32; processes and participants' roles are added) can be considered:

> *The economist and Middle East expert, Dieter Weiss,* [Sayer] *says* [process of saying] "*We see the model of an economy based on social justice, economic independence, personal responsibility and achievement*" [Verbiage]*.*

This has been translated as (processes and participants' roles are added):

> قال [process of saying] الخبير الاقتصادي المتخصص في شؤون الشرق الأوسط ديتور وييس [Sayer]: ((نحن نرى نموذجا لاقتصاد يعتمد على العدالة الاجتماعية، والاستقلال الاقتصادي، والمسؤولية الفردية، والإنجازات)) [verbage].

where قال is the Sayer, الخبير الاقتصادي المتخصص في شؤون الشرق الأوسط ديتور وييس is the process of saying, and نحن نرى نموذجا لاقتصاد يعتمد على العدالة الاجتماعية، والاستقلال الاقتصادي، والمسؤولية الفردية، والإنجازات is the Verbiage of the process.

To reinforce this, let us consider these two examples quoted from *The Scarlet Letter* by Nathaniel Hawthorne (1988) and translated by Kīwān (2007):

> "Come along, Pearl!" said she, drawing her away. "Come and look into this fair garden . . ." (p. 95).

In the above example, a verbal process is employed by the writer where:

- the pronoun *she* refers to the mother is the Sayer of the process,
- the verb *said* in the past is the process of saying,

- the non-tensed clause *drawing her away* where the pronoun *her* refers to her daughter is a manner circumstance construing the way in which the process is actualized and presented, thus answering a question of this kind "how did she say?",
- *Pearl* is the Receiver, i.e. addressee, and
- "*Come along, Pearl! Come and look into this fair garden*" is the Verbiage of the process.

Being fully aware of the process along with its participants and manner circumstance, the translator has rendered it into:

قالت وهي تجذب ابنتها بعيداً: هيا يا بيرل، تعالي وانظري إلى هذه الحديقة الجميلة.
(p. 156).

Following is the second example (p. 224):

"Is not this better", murmured he, "than what we dreamed of in the forest?"

As can be observed here, two participants are utilized by the writer in this process of saying. They are:

- the pronoun *he* is the Sayer of the process, and
- *Is not this better than what we dreamed of in the forest?* is the Verbiage of the process.

The process along with its participants has been rendered into:

تمتم قائلًا: أليس هذا أفضل مما حلمنا فيه في الغابة؟
(p. 548).

Behavioural processes

Behavioural processes (also known as processes of behaving) reflect physiological and psychological behaviours (Halliday 1994: 139; Halliday and Matthiessen [1985] 2014: 302). They can be divided into (1) processes manifesting physiological, (2) processes representing bodily postures and pastimes, (3) physiological processes manifesting states of consciousness and (4) material processes functioning as behavioural processes. Following are the common verbs that can serve as behavioural processes in both languages (Almanna 2018: 111):

- processes manifesting physiological acts, such as:
  to breathe, to cough, to yawn, to hiccup, to burp, to belch, to vomit, to sneeze, to sleep, etc.   تنفّس، سعلَ، تثاءب، فاق أو حزّق (أصيب بالفواق أو الحازوقة)، تجشأ، تقيأ أو إستقرغ، عطس، نام ...

- processes representing bodily postures and pastimes, such as:
  to sit down, to stand up, to sing, to dance, etc.   جلسَ، قامَ، غنّى، رقصَ ...

- physiological processes manifesting states of consciousness, such as: *to cry, to sob, to hiss, to laugh, to smile, to frown, to nod, to snarl, to whine, to sigh*, etc.

  بكى، نحبَ، نشجَ، حفّ، صفرَ، هسهسَ، ضحك، إبتسمَ، عبسَ، تنهّد، زفرَ، تأوّه، دمدمَ، دندنَ، زمجرَ، تأففَ، نادَ ...

- material processes functioning as behavioural processes, such as: *to chat, to talk, to murmur, to gossip, to watch, to look, to stare, to listen, to dream*, etc.

  دردش، تكلّم، تمتم، همس، اغتابَ، شاهدَ، نظر، أجال النظر في، أحدّ النظر، أطال النظر، تفرّس، حدّق، حملق، اصغى، حلِم ...

Behavioural processes usually have one participant labelled Behaver. It is a process where the Behaver, like the Senser, is a conscious being, and the process is more like one of doing. As an illustration, the following example extracted from a short story titled امرأة وحيدة *A Lonely Woman* by Zakariyyā Tāmir (translated by and cited in Husni and Newman 2008: 48–49) can be given full consideration:

ازدادت رائحة البخور وتكاثفت، وراحت عزيزة تتنفس بصوت مسموع. وهتف الشيخ سعيد فجأة: ((تعالوا تعالوا يا مباركين تعالوا)).

In this example, in راحت عزيزة تتنفس بصوت مسموع *Aziza started to breathe loudly*, a process of behaving is utilized where *Aziza* is the Behaver, تتنفس *to breathe* is the process of behaving and بصوت مسموع *loudly* is a manner circumstance construing the way in which the process is actualized and presented. As can be seen, by the effect of the verb راح, the process is characterized by multiplexity, that is, the quantity consists of more one element, thus stretching the process over time (for more details on multiplexity, as opposed to uniplexity, see Chapter 6 of this book). Being fully aware of the processes employed by the author, the translators have translated the above text as:

> *The smell of incense grew much stronger. Aziza started to breathe loudly. Sheikh Said shouted: "Come, blessed ones, come!"*

Had the translators, for instance, resorted to *Aziza breathed loudly* where the process is characterized by uniplexity, that is, the quantity consists of one element, they would have created a slightly different mental image although the process has not been changed. This indicates that, in addition to paying extra attention to the process itself along with its participants and circumstances, full consideration should be given to the characteristics of the process employed by the writer (these characteristics will be discussed in detail in Chapters 6 and 7 of this book). To reinforce this, the advertisement about an Arabic newspaper called الشرق الأوسط *Al-Sharq Al-'Awsaṭ* discussed in Chapter 3 may be reconsidered here.

In an attempt to strengthen the meaning that the advertiser tries to reflect, the slogan below is used at the bottom of the advertisement:

الجريدة الناجحة لا تتثاءب

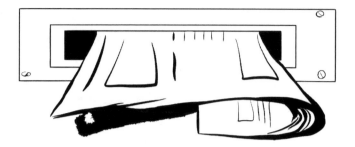

which literally means 'a successful newspaper does not yawn'. As can be seen, a behavioural process where الجريدة الناجحة *a successful newspaper* is the Behaver and تتثاءب *to yawn* in the negative form is the process of behaving. Here, there is an implicit adverb of frequency or habituality, such as *always*, that gives rise to "a habitual interpretation of simple present tense clauses" (Almanna 2016b: 66). To put this differently, we do not talk about a single event but rather a series of events of not yawning approached from a distal perspective, thus being seen as a point on the timeline.

Relational processes

Relational processes are typically realized in English by the verb *to be* or some verbs of the same class, such as *to seem, to grow, to feel, to remain, to keep, to turn, to become, to look, to sound* and the like, whose function is to model experiences in terms of being or having rather than doing, behaving, saying or sensing (Halliday and Matthiessen [1985] 2014: 106–10). In other words, these processes enable language users to characterize, describe, identify, define and classify some details of the picture conjured up in their minds. By doing so, they will be able to relate one fragment of experience to another.

When the function of the relational process is to characterize or describe, then there are two participants, viz. Carrier and Attribute. However, when the relational process is to identify or classify, then there are two participants, namely Identified and Identifier. When the two participants (Identified and Identifier) are reversible, then the relational process is a process of identifying. However, when the two participants (Carrier and Attribute) are not reversible, the relational process is attributive.

Relational processes, whether identifying or attributive, can be classified into three main types, namely

1   Process of being

   • expressed by the verb *to be* followed by an adjective, as in:

	clever	
She is/was	strong-minded	مبتدأ وخبر:
	rich	إنها/كانت...

Transitivity system **69**

- expressed by the verb *to be* followed by a noun phrase, as in:

He is/was | *a teacher*
           | *a doctor*
           | *a journalist*

مبتدأ وخبر:
إنه/كان...

2 Process of being at/in/with ...

- expressed by the verb *to be* followed by a prepositional phrase, as in:

She is/was | *at home*
           | *in the college*
           | *with her mother*

مبتدأ وخبر:
إنها/كانت...

3 Process of having

- expressed by verbs such as *to have, to own, to belong to, to possess, to include, to contain, to consist of,* etc. followed by a noun phrase or prepositional phrase, as in:

I [Possessor] *have* three children [Possessed].
My friend [Possessor] *has* a lot of money [Possessed].
The car [Possessed] *is owned* by my brother [Possessor].
The book [Possessed] *belongs to* Sara [Possessor].
This book [Possessor] *consists of* seven chapters [Possessed].

To illustrate, the following two examples extracted from Mary Ali's text titled *Women's Liberation through Islam*, published on 24 June 2013 (www.islamreligion. com) can be discussed:

A Muslim woman has the full right to approve or deny a proposal of marriage ...

As can be seen, a process of having is used by the author where *A Muslim woman* is the Carrier/Possessor; the verb *to have* is the possessive attributive process, that is, the process of having; and *the full right to approve or deny a proposal of marriage* is Attribute/Possessed. This process of having has been translated by Al-'Abrī (2015: 14) into:

تتمتع المرأة المسلمة بالحرية المطلقة لقبول عرض الزواج ورفضه ...

It is worth noting that the above process of having can be also rendered as:

للمرأة المسلمة مطلق الحرية في قبول عرض الزواج ورفضه ...

70 Transitivity system

However, in the following example, the relational process *Islam is clear* has been changed to a process of saying وضّح الإسلام *Islam explained* (Ibid.: 16):

Islam is clear in its teachings that God created men and women to be different, with unique roles, functions and skills.
وضّح الإسلام في تعاليمه أن الله قد خلق الرجل والمرأة مختلفين في الأدوار والوظائف والمهارات الفريدة.

Existential processes

Existential processes (also known as processes of existing) are typically realized by the verb *to be* or some other related verbs, such as *to exist, to remain, to arise, to occur, to happen, to take place, to come about* and the like, as in:

There + verb *to be* or some other related verbs

Existential processes typically have one obligatory participant, labelled Existent, which can represent a wide range of referents, including a thing, person, object, institution, abstraction, action and event (Halliday 1994: 106–107; Halliday and Matthiessen [1985] 2014: 142). To explain, following are two examples extracted from a political article titled *Decoding Daesh* by Alice Guthrie published on 19 February 2015 (translated by and cited in Al-Mayāhī 2016):

. . . there's something specifically important in this particular story which is being overlooked as a result of all the lazy journalism around it . . .

As can be observed, this process of existing *there's something specifically important in this particular story* where *something specifically important in this particular story* is the Existent of the process has been rendered into a process of exiting as follows:

هناك شيءٌ آخر مهم جداً في هذه القصة التي يجري التغاضي عنها نتيجة كسل وتهاون الصحافة عنه . . . (p. 22)

Following is the second example:

Over the last few months, there has been a concerted effort by several senior global politicians to give a new name to the group known as ISIS, or Islamic State.

Again, a process of existing *there has been* has been utilized by the author and reflected in the target text, as in:

في غضون الأشهر القليلة الماضية، كانت هناك جهودٌ متضافرةٌ بذلها العديد من كبار السياسيين العالميين لصياغة اسم للمجموعة التي تُعرف بالدولة الإسلامية في العراق والشام أو داعش.
(p. 33)

In studying these different types of processes, three main components should be given serious consideration. They are:

1 the *process* itself normally expressed by a verbal group,
2 the *participants* determined in advance by the writer/speaker which are typically realized by a nominal group, with the exception of some processes of being (see above), and
3 the *circumstances* associated with the process typically expressed by an adverb or a prepositional phrase.

Circumstances

Having studied the processes along with their participants, whether obligatory or optional, adequate consideration is given to the circumstances that may be employed by the language user (be it writer or speaker) to provide their readers/hearers with extra information on the time, place, manner and reason of the process. Following Halliday (1994; also discussed in Almanna 2018: 118–123), circumstances can be classified as follows:

- **Location circumstances** construe the extent of the unfolding of the process in space and/or time and answer the questions 'when' or 'where', as in:

  | Temporal | # *Last year*, I travelled to the UK. | When? |
  | Spatial | # I have lived *in London* for two years. | Where? |

- **Extent circumstances**, like location circumstances, construe the extent of the unfolding of the process in space and/or time but answer questions like 'for how long', 'how far' or 'how many times', as in:

Duration	# I have slept *for an hour*.	For how long?
Distance	# I drove *20 miles* yesterday.	How far?
Frequency	# I visit my family *three times a year*.	How many times?

- **Manner circumstances** construe the way in which the process is actualized and presented, thus answering questions like 'how', 'by what means', 'what like', or 'how much', as in:

72 Transitivity system

    Quality   # He threw the ball to his friend <u>strongly</u>.   How?/With what?
    Means   # He opened the door <u>with a tea spoon</u>.   By what means?
    Comparison # Try to do your job <u>as professionally as</u> you can.   How?
    Degree   # All his friends love him <u>deeply</u>.   How much?

- **Cause circumstances** construe the reason, in its boarder sense, why the process is actualized, thus answering the questions 'why', 'for what purpose' and 'on whose behalf/who for', as in:

    Reason   # I have left early <u>as I have a lot of things to do</u>.   Why?
    Purpose # I went to the mall <u>to buy a new laptop</u>.   For what purpose?
    Behalf   # He said sorry <u>on behalf of his son</u>.   On whose behalf?

- **Contingency circumstances** specify certain elements on which the actualization of the process depends, with the sense of *if* (representing positive cases of condition), with the sense of *if not* (representing negative cases of condition) and with the sense of *although* (representing cases of concession).

    Condition   # <u>In case of emergency</u>, the students can leave the exam room and go to the WC.
    Default   # <u>In the absence of the teacher</u>, the head of the department can ask any teacher to cover him/her.
    Concession # <u>Despite his illness</u>, he has managed to complete his studies.

- **Accompaniment circumstances** are forms of joint participation in the process and answer questions like 'with whom' and 'without whom', as in:

    Company   # She goes to school <u>with her dad</u>.   With whom?
    Lack of company # She can live in this city <u>without him</u>.   Without whom?

- **Role circumstances** construe the meanings *to be* and *to become* circumstantially, thus answering the question 'what as' and 'what into', as in:

    Guise   # I have worked <u>as a translator</u> for many years.   What as?
    Product # She cut the cake <u>into many small pieces</u>.   What into?

- **Matter circumstances** can be replaced in verbal processes with the Verbiage of the process. Matter circumstances are typically expressed by prepositions, such as *about, concerning, regarding, with reference to, with respect to, as for* and the like, thus answering a like 'what about', as in:

    Focusing   # Do not think <u>about these silly issues</u> if you want to ease your mind.   What about?

- **Angle circumstances** can represent the Sayer's source of information in verbal processes with the sense of 'as ... says', typically expressed by complex prepositions, such as *according to, in the words of* and the like, thus answering the questions 'according to whom'. Similarly, angle circumstances can represent the Senser's viewpoint in mental processes with the sense of 'as ... thinks', typically expressed by the simple preposition *to* or complex prepositions, such as *from the standpoint of, in the opinion of, in the view of, to one's mind, in one's book*, and so on, as in:

Source	# <u>According to our teacher</u>, we are not allowed to use dictionaries.	According to whom?
Viewpoint	# It seems <u>to me</u> she won't come to the party.	What's your opinion?

To show how (not) paying extra attention to the circumstances employed by the writer may affect the translation accuracy, the following example extracted from a collection of poems titled إن القنابل لم تفطر الآن *Bombs Have Not Breakfasted Yet* by 'Adnān Al-Sā'īgh (translated by and cited in Kadhim and Sullivan [2013: 40–41]) may be considered:

أصعدني الحلاج ُ إلى أعلى تلٍ
في بغداد
وأراني كل مآذنها ومعابدها

Al-Hallaj lifted me to the highest hill in all Baghdad
to show me its minarets and temples

Here, two processes are employed by the poet. They are أصعدني *he lifted me* and أراني *he showed me*. These two processes are characterized by having a force value where one (powerful) participant enables the other (powerless or dependent) participant to go up the highest hill in Baghdad and see its minarets and temples (for more details on force dynamics, see Chapter 7 of this book).

To speed up the pace of events, the poet decides to join these two processes by the connector و *and*. However, the second process, as can be observed, has been changed by the translators to a cause circumstance that construes the reason for going up to the highest hill in Baghdad. In the source text, it is asserted that Al-Hallaj showed him the minarets and temples as the emphasis is placed on the completion of the act of showing in a specific period in the past. Building on this, the extent of causation is greater than the scope of intention. However, by the effect of the non-finite clause of purpose introduced by *to*, the scope of intention becomes greater than the extent of causation in the target text, thereby creating a different mental image. Had the translators given these issues serious consideration, they could have suggested a rendering of the following kind *and showed me its minarets and temples*.

To clarify this point, the following text extracted from a short story titled صفحة من كتاب الموتى *Excerpt from The Book of The Dead* by Ibrāhīm Al-Faqīh (translated by and cited in Husni and Newman 2008: 86–87) may be considered:

عاد من جديد يسترق النظر إليها عله يجد شيئاً في ملامحها يضيء ما اعتراه من حيرة وذهول.
Once again he glanced over at her, and noticed something in her features that shed light on what had baffled him.

74 Transitivity system

Here, a process of behaving is utilized by the writer where the implicit pronoun هو *he* is the Behaver and استرق النظر *to glance over* is the process of behaving. By virtue of عاد من جديد, the process is characterized by multiplexity, that is, عاد يسترق النظر refers to a series of acts of glancing, not a single act. The translators have reflected the process but failed to reflect its characteristics. Further, by the effect of عله used in the source text, the scope of intention is greater than the extent of causation. However, in the target text, the translators have imposed different specifications on the scene when they have opted for the additive connector *and*, thereby emphasizing the completion of the act of noticing in a specific point in the past. Had the translators given adequate consideration to:

a   the process of behaving and its characteristics, and
b   the scope of intention and extent of causation in عله يجد شيئاً.

they would have suggested a rendering, such as *Once again he started glancing over at her in an attempt to notice something in her features that shed light on what had baffled him.*

Now, let us discuss the following text adapted from a short story titled القطار الصاعد إلى بغداد *The Train Heading up to Baghdad* by Maḥmūd ʿAbdulwahhāb (translated by and cited in Pragnell and Sadkhan 2011: 11):

عندما صفر القطار صفرته الثانية الحادة المتقطعة فكَّت أمي عقدة فوطتها وسلَّمتني الدينار الوحيد الذي تملكه . . .

When the train gave its second, sharp shrill whistle, my mother untied the knot of her apron and gave me the only dinar she had . . .

Here, two main material processes along with an adverbial subordinate clause are employed by the writer. By virtue of عندما *when*, which can be replaced in this context with في اللحظة *the moment*, حالما *once* and so on, and the additive connector و *and* that joins these two main material processes, the pace of events is sped up, thus indicating there is no time lapse among the processes, as modelled below:

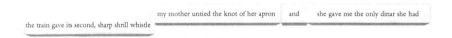

To begin with, عندما صفر القطار صفرته الثانية الحادة المتقطعة *when the train gave its second, sharp shrill whistle* is an adverbial subordinate clause construing the extent of the unfolding of the process in space and time, thus answering the questions 'When did she untie the knot of her apron?' and 'When did she give her son the only dinar she had?' As for فكَّت أمي عقدة فوطتها *my mother untied the knot of her apron*, it is a material process where أمي *my mother* is the Actor of the process and عقدة فوطتها *the knot of her apron* is the Goal of the process. In سلمتني الدينار الوحيد الذي عقدة فوطتها

تملكه *she gave me the only dinar that she had*, another material process is employed by the writer where the implicit pronoun هي *she* is the Actor, the pronoun ني *me* is the Recipient of the process and الدينار الوحيد *the only dinar* is the Goal of the process. In this material process, an embedded process of having is utilized to modify the Goal of the process. Although the morphological tense in this process is in the present tense تملك, the emphasis is placed on its completion as there is an implicit كان which implies past. Having given full consideration to the processes along with their participants and circumstances, and the speed of pace of the events and time lapse, the translators have managed to produce an accurate and adequate translation. Had the translators opted for different grammatical forms, such as:

After the train had given its second, sharp shrill whistle, my mother untied the knot of her apron. Then, she gave me the only dinar she had . . .

they would have reflected the processes along with their participants and circumstances but created time gaps among the processes, thus affecting the mental image(s).

In the following example extracted from a novel titled بنات الرياض *Girls of Riyadh* by Rajā' Al-Ṣāni' (2007: 5; also discussed in Mshari 2016: 79 from a different perspective) and translated by Alsanea and Booth (2008: 2), a material process is employed by the writer:

تسير سديم خلف صديقتها محنية الظهر خوفاً من أن تظهر في الصور . . .

Behind her, Sadeem followed her progress with utter concentration, ducking to avoid appearing in any of the photos . . .

In this material process two circumstances are employed. They are:

- محنية الظهر *ducking*, a manner circumstance construing the way in which the process is actualized and presented, thus answering the question 'How did she walk?'
- خوفاً من أن تظهر في الصور *for fear she might appear in any of the photos*, a cause circumstance construing the reason why she walked in that way.

As can be noticed, these two circumstances have been reflected by the translators when opting for *ducking to avoid appearing in any of the photos*. However, for no obvious reason, they have added another circumstance, that is, *with utter concentration*, thereby creating a slightly different mental image.

76 Transitivity system

To discuss the effect of changing the process or its elements on the mental image conjured up in our minds, these two examples extracted from *BBC* (23 October 2017) can be examined:

> *According to Ekho Moskvy, the alleged attacker's name is Boris Grits. It describes the attacker as an Israeli, citing 'informed sources'.*
> وقالت إذاعة إيكو موسكوفي إن منفذ الهجوم هو بوريس غريتس، ووصفته بأنه إسرائيلي الجنسية، وفقا لما أطلقت عليه 'مصادر مطلعة'.

As we may observe, the angle circumstance *according to Ekho Moskvy* that represents the Sayer's source of information, thus indicating an implicit verbal process, is replaced with an explicit verbal process قالت إذاعة إيكو موسكوفي. Although the type of the sentence is changed from a simple sentence in English to a complex one in Arabic and, accordingly, the process of being becomes the Verbiage of the verbal process in Arabic (see below), the mental image has not been affected dramatically as explained below:

> *According to Ekho Moskvy* [an angle circumstance], *the alleged attacker's name is Boris Grits* [process of being].
> قالت [a process of saying] إذاعة إيكو موسكوفي [Sayer] إن منفذ الهجوم هو بوريس غريتس
> [process of being as a Verbiage]

Following is the second example:

> *The knifeman reportedly sprayed a gas into the face of a security guard as he broke in.*
> وقالت تقارير إن الرجل الذي كان يحمل سكينا باغت حارس الأمن برش غاز في وجهه واقتحم مبنى الإذاعة لتنفيذ الهجوم.

In the above example, the adverb *reportedly* in the material process is changed to a verbal process ... إن قالت تقارير, which roughly means *reports said that* .... Despite that, such a shift in the processes has not changed the mental image conjured up in our mind as the adverb *reportedly* indicates an implicit verbal process. Further, in the Verbiage of the verbal process in Arabic the Actor of the material process, that is, الرجل *the man*, is modified by a relative clause الذي كان يحمل سكيناً *who was carrying a knife*. Such a process added in the Arabic version has not changed the mental image conjured up in our mind because by the effect of the grammatical form employed by *BBC* in its English version, that is, *the knifeman*, we still see in our mind's eye the man carrying a knife in both versions (for more details on this example, see the next chapter).

Now, let us line up these two *BBC* news items touching on the same topic (one in English and the other in Arabic; 25 April 2016) to discuss the processes utilized in both versions:

> *Riot police* [Actor] *have fired tear gas and birdshot* [Goal] *to disperse anti-government protesters in Egypt's capital, Cairo.*

أطلقت الشرطة المصرية [Actor] قنابل الغاز المسيل للدموع [Goal] لتفريق محتجين على اتفاقية مصرية سعودية تنتقل بمقتضاها السيادة على جزيرتي تيران وصنافير إلى السعودية.

Here, a material process is employed by *BBC* where:

- *riot police* ^^ الشرطة المصرية is the Actor of the process,
- *tear gas and birdshot* ^^ قنابل الغاز المسيل للدموع is the Goal of the process, and
- *anti-government protesters* ^^ محتجين على اتفاقية مصرية سعودية is the Recipient of the process.

In this process, an open path is recruited where the starting point (where the police stand) and endpoint (where the protesters stand) are different. Further, the interaction between the police and protesters is construed as unidirectional based on an asymmetrical action schema where the transfer of energy flows from the Agent (the police) to the Affected Participant (the protesters) (for more details on energy transfer, see the next chapter). This has been reflected in both versions. However, the word *birdshot* has been added by *BBC* in its English version or it might be deleted in its Arabic version. Such an addition or omission has not only influenced the mental image conjured up in the reader/hearer's mind but also provides them with a different interpretive frame. This new interpretive frame may change their responses to the narrative at hand (Almanna 2016a: 202). By doing so, the translator or trans-editor becomes an active participant in reframing realities.

Let us shift our focus towards the circumstance used with the process. As can be observed, the non-finite clause of purpose introduced by *to* in English and ل in Arabic is a cause circumstance construing the reason why the process is actualized, thus answering the question 'For what purpose have the police fired tear gas (and birdshot)?'. It is worth noting that in this non-finite clause of purpose, it is not asserted that the police have succeeded in dispersing the protesters. To put this differently, the scope of intention is greater than the extent of causation. This has been reflected in both texts. However, the reason behind protesting, i.e. to protest against an Egyptian-Saudi agreement in which Tiran and Sanafir islands were transferred to Saudi Arabia, has been explicitly expressed by *BBC* in its Arabic version, while it has been reduced in its English version to *anti-government protesters*. Again, such a local strategy adopted by *BBC* has provided the reader of the Arabic version with a different narrative.

To finish off this chapter, the following advertisement for a type of Patek Philippe watch called Twenty~4, discussed in Chapter 2 of this book, can be examined here from a different perspective. The English version pictures a female model called Bridget Hall wearing the advertised watch. In addition to the slogan in which a relational process is recruited *Who will you be in the 24 hours?*, a number of processes can be interpreted, namely an existential process *There is an attractive girl*, a relational process *She looks sexy*, a relational process *She is ready to go out*, a behavioural process *She is looking somewhere*, a possessive attributive process *She wears a watch*, a behavioural process *She is sitting on a bed*, an existential process *There is a watch*, as well as others. Here, the woman, the represented participant, is depicted from a low angle, that is, she is viewed from below. This indicates that the represented participant, the woman, is in a position of power, thus indicating her strength and other related qualities.

78 Transitivity system

Who will you be in the next 24 hours?

    This is another implicit message sent out by the advertiser stating that when you buy and wear this watch, you will be as strong as this model.

    In the Arabic version, apart from the two relational processes, i.e. *She looks sexy* and *She is ready to go out*, the other processes employed in the English version have been reflected. To elaborate, in addition to the slogan in which a relation process is recruited من ستكونين في ال ٢٤ ساعة المقبلة؟, a number of processes can be figured out: *There is an attractive girl* (existential process), *She is looking somewhere* (behavioural process), *She wears a watch* (possessive attributive process), *She is sitting on a sofa* (behavioural process), *There is a watch* (existential process) and so on. Here, the model is depicted from a low angle, thus indicating her strength and other related qualities. The implicit message sent out by the advertiser in the English version, i.e. when you buy and wear this watch, you will be as strong as this model, has been reflected by the translator.

من ستكونين في الـ ٢٤ ساعة المقبلة؟

Key technical terms

- Actor
- Behaver
- Behavioural process (process of behaving)
- Carrier
- Existential

- Existential process (process of existing)
- Happening process
- Material process (process of doing)
- Mental process (process of sensing)

Transitivity system **79**

- Relational process (process of being/having)
- Sayer
- Senser
- Transitivity
- Verbal process (process of saying)
- Verbiage

Exercises

Exercise 1: Identify the processes along with their participants and circumstances in the following examples written for the purpose of this course. Then, translate them into English, giving full consideration to the mental image conjured up in your mind:

\# إن الرَّجلَ الذي يضحكُ هناك هو والدي.
\# ثمة العديد من المشاكل العالقة التي تنتظر حلًّا جذرياً بين البلدين.
\# ما إن لمحها من بعيد حتى غمرته السعادة وذهبَ إليها مسرعًا.
\# بعثَ أحدُ أصدقائي المقرّبين رسالة إلى إحدى الجامعات مستفسرًا عن الوظيفة الشاغرة.
\# يملك العديد من البيوت والشقق في وسط المدينة، لكنه يشعر بحزن شديد بعد أن سافر ابنه إلى المملكة المتحدة لإكمال دراستهِ.

Exercise 2: The following three texts are extracted from *The Scarlet Letter* by Nathaniel Hawthorne (1988) and translated by Kīwān (2007). Your task is to

a identify the processes along with their participants and circumstances, and
b compare the processes used in the original text with those employed by the translator.

1	*She hath good skill at her needle, that's certain* ... (p. 49)	إنها تمتلك مهارة جيدة في الخياطة ... (p. 22)
2	*"I can teach my little Pearl what I have learned from this!" answered Hester Prynne, laying her finger on the red token.* (p. 98)	أجابت أستير برين وهي تضع إصبعاً على الرمز الأحمر: أستطيع أن أعلم طفلتي بيرل ما تعلمته أنا من هذا! (p. 168)
3	*There is truth in what she says* ... (p. 101)	توجد حقيقة فيما تقوله ... (p. 178)

Exercise 3: In the following text taken from a novel titled بنات الرياض *Girls of Riyadh* by Rajā' Al-Ṣāni' (2007: 17), two material processes, namely توجهن *they headed* ... and اشترين *they bought* ... are employed by the author. Comment on the processes in the target text (Alsanea and Booth 2008: 25):

They headed for a tiny shop that sold water pipes, or what we call the shisha – otherwise known as hookah or hubby. The girls bought enough shisha that they would not have to share ...	توجهن إلى محل صغير لبيع الشيشة والجراك والمعسل واشترين شيشاً بعددهن ...

80 Transitivity system

Exercise 4: Read the following *BBC* news items touching on the same topic (23 October 2017) to identify the processes employed in both versions. Then, comment on the time lapse between the processes used in both versions:

| One of the broadcaster's security guards was injured as the knifeman was being overpowered. | وأصيب في الهجوم أحد حراس الأمن في الإذاعة أثناء محاولة السيطرة على المسلح. |

Exercise 5: The following text is taken from a collection of poems titled إن القنابل لم تفطر الآن *Bombs Have Not Breakfasted Yet* by 'Adnān Al-Ṣā'īgh and translated by Kadhim and Sullivan (2013: 56–57; bilingual edn). Identify the types of processes used in both texts, then comment on the translation.

A lame man looked at the sky	نظرَ الأعرجُ إلى السماء	Process of _____
and cried out	وهتف بغضبٍ	Process of _____
Lord,	أيها الربُّ	
If you did not possess enough clay	إن لم يكن لديك طينٌ كافٍ	Process of _____
why rush to create me?	فعلامَ تعجّلتَ في تكويني	Process of _____

Further reading

Almanna, A. (2018). *The Nuts and Bolts of Arabic-English Translation: An Introduction to Applied Contrastive Linguistics.* Newcastle upon Tyne, England: Cambridge Scholars Publishing.
Goodman, S. (1996). "Visual English". In S. Goodman and D. Graddol (eds.), *Redesigning English: New Text, New Identities.* London/New York: Routledge.
Halliday, M. A. K. (1976). "Notes on Transitivity and Theme in English: Part 2", *Journal of Linguistics,* Vol. 3 (1), pp. 199–244.
———. (1994). *An Introduction to Functional Grammar* (2nd edn). London et al.: Arnold.
Halliday, M. A. K. and Matthiessen, C. M. I. M. ([1985] 2014). *Halliday's Introduction to Functional Grammar* (4th edn). London/New York: Routledge.
———. (1999). *Construing Experience Through Meaning: A Language-Based Approach to Cognition.* London/New York: Cassell.
Kress, G. and van Leeuwen, T. (1996). *Reading Images: The Grammar of Visual Design.* London/New York: Routledge.
Matthiessen, C. M. I. M. (1976). *Ways of Paradox and Other Essays* (Revised in enlarger edn). Cambridge, MA: Harvard University Press.
———. (1992). *Pursuit of Truth* (2nd edn). Cambridge, MA: Harvard University Press.
———. (1995). *Lexicogrammatical Cartography: English Systems.* Tokyo: International Language Sciences.
———. (2004). *An Introduction to Functional Grammar* (3rd edn). London et al.: Arnold.

References

Al-'Abrī, S. (2015). *Translating and Annotating Ideology-loaded Texts: 'Women Liberation Through Islam' and 'Thirty Facts About Islam' as Samples.* BA final Year Project. Oman: University of Nizwa.

Ali, M. (2013). *Women's Liberation Through Islam*. Accessed on 24 June 2015: <www. islam-religion.com>.

Almanna, A. (2016a). *The Routeldge Course in Translation Annotation: Arabic-English-Arabic*. London/New York: Routledge.

———. (2016b). *Semantics for Translation Students: Arabic-English-Arabic*. Oxford: Peter Lang.

———. (2018). *The Nuts and Bolts of Arabic-English Translation: An Introduction to Applied Contrastive Linguistics*. Newcastle upon Tyne, England: Cambridge Scholars Publishing.

Al-Mayā<u>h</u>ī, H. (2016). *Decoding and Translating Daesh with a Focus on Vinay and Darblnet's (1958/1995) Local Strategies and Catford's (1965) Shift Theory*. BA final Year Project. Oman: University of Nizwa.

Alsanea, R. and Booth, M. (trans.) (2008). *Girls of Riyadh*. New York: Penguin Press.

Al-Sāni', R. (2007). بنات الرياض *'Girls of Riyadh'*. Beirut: Saqi Books.

Al-<u>S</u>huraīqī, M. (2016). *Translating Hans Küng's Book 'Islam: Past, Present and Future' and Annotating the Local Strategies Adopted*. BA final Year Project. Oman: University of Nizwa.

Goodman, S. (1996). "Visual English". In S. Goodman and D. Graddol (eds.), *Redesigning English: New Text, New Identities*. London/New York: Routledge.

Halliday, M. A. K. (1976). "Notes on Transitivity and Theme in English: Part 2", *Journal of Linguistics*, Vol. 3 (1), pp. 199–244.

———. (1994). *An Introduction to Functional Grammar* (2nd edn). London et al.: Arnold.

Halliday, M. A. K. and Matthiessen, C. M. I. M. ([1985] 2014). *Halliday's Introduction to Functional Grammar* (4th edn). London/New York: Routledge.

———. (1999). *Construing Experience Through Meaning: A Language-Based Approach to Cognition*. London/New York: Cassell.

Hawthorne, N. (1988). *The Scarlet Letter*. Beirut: York Press.

Husni, R. and Newman, D. (2008; bilingual edn). *Modern Arabic Short Stories: A Binigual Reader*. London: Saqi Books.

Kadhim, A. and Sullivan, D. (2013; bilingual edn). إن القنابل لم تفطر الآن *Bombs Have Not Breakfasted Yet*. London: Iraqi Cultural Centre.

Kīwān, A. (trans.) (2007). الحرف القرمزي. Beirut: Dār Al-Bi<u>h</u>ār.

Kress, G. and van Leeuwen, T. (1996). *Reading Images: The Grammar of Visual Design*. London/New York: Routledge.

Matthiessen, C. M. I. M. (1976). *Ways of Paradox and Other Essays* (Revised in enlarger edn). Cambridge, MA: Harvard University Press.

———. (1992). *Pursuit of Truth* (2nd edn). Cambridge, MA: Harvard University Press.

———. (1995). *Lexicogrammatical Cartography: English Systems*. Tokyo: International Language Sciences.

———. (2004). *An Introduction to Functional Grammar* (3rd edn). London et al.: Arnold.

Mshari, A. F. (2016). *Translation Shifts in Rajaa Alsanea's Novel Girls of Riyadh: A Text Linguistic Perspective*, unpublished M.A. thesis: Basrah University.

Pragnell, F. and Sadkhan, R. (2011). *Ten Stories from Iraq: A Bilingual Reader*. London: Sayyab Books Ltd.

Sadkhan, R. and Pragnell, F. (2012). رائحة الشتاء *The Scent of Winter: A Bilingual Reader*. London: Sayyab Books Ltd.

Simpson, P. (1993). *Language, Ideology and Point of View*. London/New York: Routledge.

5
SEMANTIC ROLES AND FLOW OF ENERGY

The previous chapter discussed the transitivity system and the main processes that may be used by the language users to reflect the world around them along with their participants and circumstances. It highlighted the importance of paying extra attention to reflecting these processes along with their participants and circumstances in the target text as often as we can. This chapter gives full consideration to the semantic roles (also known as 'thematic roles', 'theta roles' and 'semantic cases') assigned to each noun phrase (also called 'argument') in the clause. It is held in this chapter that in order to create a similar mental image in our readers' minds, adequate consideration should be given to these semantic roles filled by each argument.

Arguments and types of semantic roles

In any process (be it material, mental, behavioural, verbal, existent, etc.), there is a verb (explicit or implicit, depending on the language) and a noun phrase (or more, depending on the verb itself) that describes the role that the entity has with the main verb in a certain clause. In a sentence like this:

With the knife, the thief killed the woman.

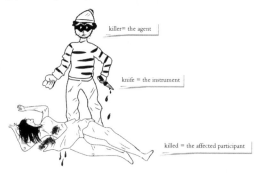

Semantic roles and flow of energy **83**

a material process is expressed where there is a verb describing an action (i.e. killing the woman), and three arguments filling different semantic roles, as follows:
- *the thief* fills a semantic role of Agent, that is, the initiator of the act of killing who is responsible for his/her decision,
- *the woman* fills a semantic role of Affected Participant, that is, it describes the entity that undergoes an action and changes its state, and
- *the knife* fills a semantic role of Instrument, that is, it describes the entity with which the Agent (*the thief*) did the act of killing.

However, in a sentence like this:

My daughter saw a man in the street.

a mental process is utilized where there is a verb describing a mental process (i.e. seeing a man) and three arguments, viz.:

- *my daughter* fills the role of Experiencer, that is, it describes the entity that perceives a particular mental or emotional process or state,
- *a man* fills the role of Theme, that is, it describes the entity that is perceived or, more accurately, seen without being affected by the act of seeing that does not require a physical action, and
- *in the street* fills the role of Location, that is, the semantic role that identifies the location of an entity.

It is worth noting that the entity that fills a semantic role of Theme in such a process can be sometimes affected. But what type of effect is caused? To address this question, the following example can be discussed:

The teacher saw one of his students cheat in the exam.

In this mental process, *one of his students* filling a semantic role of Theme is affected somehow, but s/he does not change his/her state or appearance as the effect is a psychological effect, hence the difference between Theme and Patient (see below).

Following several writers (e.g. Saeed 1997/2003: 149–150; Thakur 1999: 67–75; Löbner 2002: 111–113; Almanna 2016b: 126–128, among others), the main semantic roles can be summarized here as follows where the relevant role-bearing argument is underlined and labelled.

Agent The role of an argument referring to an entity that performs an action deliberately or accidently but affecting another entity, as in:
My son [Agent] *broke the glass.*
The woman was killed by the man [Agent] *yesterday morning.*

84 Semantic roles and flow of energy

	# *The cleaner* [Agent] *cleaned the house.*
	# *The thief* [Agent] *stole the man's wallet.*
	# *The cat* [Agent] *ate the eggs.*
Actor	The role of an argument that performs an action without affecting another entity, as in:
	# *The teacher* [Actor] *left the door of his office open.*
	# *My sister* [Actor] *gave me some money some days ago.*
Theme	The role of an argument that undergoes the action but does not change its state, as in:
	# *My young son saw a fly* [Theme] *on the wall.*
	# *The teacher gave the book* [Theme] *to his students.*
	# *The car* [Theme] *is outside.*
	# *The class* [Theme] *is full of students.*
Affected Participant (Patient)	The role of an argument that undergoes an action and changes its state because of another entity or due to the described event, as in:
	# *The ball broke the window* [Affected Participant].
	# *My little boy cracked the mirror* [Affected Participant] *while he was playing with his sister.*
	# *The door* [Affected Participant] *was broken by the wind.*
	# *The ice* [Affected Participant] *was melted by the sun.*
	# *The eggs* [Affected Participant] *were eaten by the dog.*
	# *The man* [Affected Participant] *was assassinated in the centre of the city.*
	# *One of my close friends* [Affected Participant] *passed away some days ago.*
Experiencer	The role of an argument that perceives a particular mental or emotional process or state, as in:
	# *I* [Experiencer] *feel hungry.*
	# *Peter* [Experiencer] *heard the door shut.*
	# *Yesterday, my young daughter* [Experiencer] *forgot her mobile in her friend's house.*
	# *The scene frightened me* [Experiencer].
Affecting Participant (Stimulus)	The role of an argument that refers to the identity that is perceived or experienced, thus affecting another entity without any action, as in:
	# *My son likes playing football* [Affecting Participant].
	# *Going out* [Affecting Participant] *delights her.*
	# *My uncle was pleased by his son's success* [Affecting Participant].
	# *These programmes* [Affecting Participant] *scared my young daughter.*
Instrument	The role of an argument with which the agent performs the action, as in:
	# *The two parties signed the contract with the same pen* [Instrument].
	# *My father locked the door with the key* [Instrument].
	# *The thief broke the window with a hammer* [Instrument].
	# *My young daughter ate the rice with the spoon* [Instrument].

Semantic roles and flow of energy **85**

Location (Locative)	The role of an argument that identifies the location of an entity, as in: # *The cat was hiding <u>under the chair</u>* [Location]. # *Your keys are <u>on the table</u>* [Location]. # *The teacher put the marker <u>on the desk</u>* [Location].
Source	The role of an argument that tells the starting point of an entity (i.e. the starting point from which it moves), as in: # *I borrowed some money from <u>my close friend</u>* [Source]. # *My father will travel tomorrow from <u>Muscat</u>* [Source] *to Basra.* # *The train came back from <u>Newcastle</u>* [Source]. # *She got the idea of her project from <u>her teacher</u>* [Source].
Goal	The role of an argument that refers to the endpoint of a process (i.e. the endpoint to which an entity moves), as in: # *John handed the parcel to <u>the man</u>* [Goal]. # *The teacher went <u>home</u>* [Goal] *early.* # *I sent a number of emails to <u>the university</u>* [Goal] *yesterday.*
Path	The role of an argument that is the pathway of a motion and through which an entity moves, as in: # *Yesterday, I walked home through <u>the narrow street</u>* [Path]. # *They drove through <u>the desert</u>* [Path]. # *I normally go to college through <u>the park</u>* [Path].
Recipient	The role of an argument that names the receiver of the entity, as in: # *<u>Tom</u>* [Recipient] *borrowed 100$ from his sister.* # *<u>One of the students</u>* [Recipient] *received a gift from his teacher.* # *My friend has sent <u>me</u>* [Recipient] *a great number of emails recently.*
Benefactor (Beneficiary)	The role of an argument that names the benefactor of the action, as in: # *Sara gave me the gift for <u>my young daughter</u>* [Benefactor]. # *My sister filled in the application form for <u>me</u>* [Benefactor]. # *I will buy <u>you</u>* [Benefactor] *a sports car.* # *My mother baked a cake for <u>us</u>* [Benefactor].
Causer	The role of an argument that is directly involved in the causation of an event, as in: # *<u>The wind</u>* [Causer] *broke the window.* # *The harvest was destroyed by <u>the heavy rain</u>* [Causer]. # *The village was inundated by <u>water</u>* [Causer]. # *Many houses were destroyed by <u>the tornado</u>* [Causer].
Resultant (Effect)	The role of an argument that comes into existence as a result of the agent's action, as in: # *Sara painted <u>a picture</u>* [Resultant]. # *I will make <u>an omelette</u>* [Resultant] *for you.* # *My mother baked <u>a pie</u>* [Resultant] *for me.*

Predicate (Associate)	The role of an argument that tells the status of another argument, as in: # My friend's car is <u>expensive</u> [Predicate]. # My sister is <u>an English teacher</u> [Predicate].
Positioner	The role of an argument that refers to an entity (a living being) that is in a stationary situation of his/her own free will, as in: # <u>The teacher</u> [Positioner] is sitting on the chair right now. # <u>My father</u> [Positioner] is lying in bed. # <u>My sister</u> [Positioner] had stayed in a hotel till yesterday.
Possessor	The role of an argument that identifies the possessor of another entity, as in: # <u>Peter's</u> [Possessor] car is very expensive. # I found <u>the teacher's</u> [Possessor] book. # <u>My brother</u> [Possessor] has three cars. # This book belongs to <u>Tom</u> [Possessor].
Accompaniment	The role of an argument that describes an entity that participates with another entity, as in: # I went with <u>my brother</u> [Accompaniment] to the mall. # Sara travelled to the UK with <u>her dad</u> [Accompaniment].
Integrant	The role of an argument with which the resultant comes into existence or the participant is affected, as in: # I sweetened the tea with <u>sugar</u> [Integrant]. # By mixing <u>floor, fat, eggs and sugar</u> [Integrant], my mother made a cake for me.

Verb-specific semantic roles

These semantic roles discussed above can be further classified into verb-specific semantic roles, that is to say, semantic roles that can be derived from the verb itself (Almanna 2018: 12). By way of explanation, let us discuss this sentence.

The teacher gave one of his best students a gift.

- *the teacher* fills a verb-specific semantic role of Giver,
- *one of his best students* fills a verb-specific semantic role of Receiver, and
- *a gift* fills a verb-specific semantic role of sth Given.

In the above example, a process of doing is employed by the language user where the emphasis, by the effect of the simple past tense, is placed on the completion of the process. In our mind's eye (represented in these two pictures quoted from Almanna 2018: 12), we can see that what was given was first with the teacher and then with one of the students. We can also see that what was given was not affected at the moment of giving the gift (it might be affected later), but it was moved from the Source (the teacher) to the Goal (one of the students).

Semantic roles and flow of energy   87

As the starting point and endpoint are not the same, it is an open path (for more details on the types of paths, see Chapter 7 of this book). To put it differently, an open path with gapping over the initial and medial portions is utilized, as modelled here:

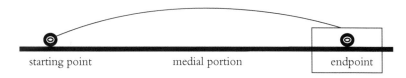

In a sentence like

John received an email from Peter.

- *John* is the person who received an email, so he fills a semantic role of Recipient and a verb-specific semantic role of Receiver,
- *an email* is what was received, so it fills a semantic role of Theme and a verb-specific role of sth Received, and
- *Peter* is the person who sent the email, so he fills a semantic role of Agent/Actor and a verb-specific semantic role of Sender.

Compare it with a sentence like this:

Peter sent an email to John.

In this example:

- *Peter* is the person who sent the email, so he fills a semantic role of Agent/Actor and a verb-specific semantic role of Sender,
- *an email* is what was sent, so it fills a semantic role of Theme and a verb-specific semantic role of sth Sent, and
- *John* is the person who received the email, so he fills a semantic role of Recipient and a verb-specific semantic role of Receiver.

In these two sentences, *John received an email from Peter* and *Peter sent an email to John*, an open path is utilized as the starting point and endpoint are different. In this open path employed in both sentences, the Source is *Peter* and the Goal is *John*. With this in mind, we can add other semantic roles to *Peter* and *John*, which are Source and Goal respectively. This fits hand in glove with Jackendoff (1990), who suggests that an argument can fulfil more than one semantic role. In his theory of tiers of semantic roles, Jackendoff proposes two tiers: (1) a thematic tier where the emphasis is placed on spatial relations and (2) an action tier where the emphasis is shifted towards the act and its effect (Ibid.). By way of explanation, let us discuss the examples adapted from him (1990: 126–127; emphasis added):

Bill [thematic tier: **Theme**, action tier: **Actor**] *hit Fred* [thematic tier: **Goal**, action tier: **Patient**]·
Bill [thematic tier: **Source**, action tier: **Actor**] *threw the ball* [thematic tier: **Goal**, action tier: **Patient**]·
Bill [thematic tier: **Theme**, action tier: **Actor**] *entered the room* [thematic tier: **Goal**, action tier: **Ø**]·
Bill [thematic tier: **Goal**, action tier: **Ø**] *received a letter* [thematic tier: **Theme**, action tier: **Ø**]·

Now let us compare the following sentences:

Bill received a letter from Kim.
Bill was sent a letter by Kim.
Kim sent a letter to Bill.
Kim sent Bill a letter.

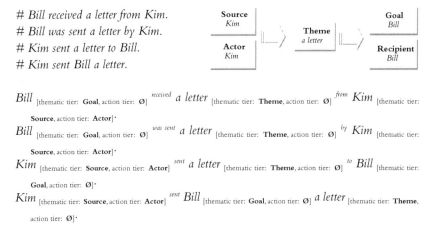

Bill [thematic tier: **Goal**, action tier: **Ø**] *received a letter* [thematic tier: **Theme**, action tier: **Ø**] *from Kim* [thematic tier: **Source**, action tier: **Actor**]·

Bill [thematic tier: **Goal**, action tier: **Ø**] *was sent a letter* [thematic tier: **Theme**, action tier: **Ø**] *by Kim* [thematic tier: **Source**, action tier: **Actor**]·

Kim [thematic tier: **Source**, action tier: **Actor**] *sent a letter* [thematic tier: **Theme**, action tier: **Ø**] *to Bill* [thematic tier: **Goal**, action tier: **Ø**]·

Kim [thematic tier: **Source**, action tier: **Actor**] *sent Bill* [thematic tier: **Goal**, action tier: **Ø**] *a letter* [thematic tier: **Theme**, action tier: **Ø**]·

As can be observed, although these four sentences are syntactically different, they convey the same idea. This is because each argument (*Bill*, *a letter* and *Kim*) carries the same semantic role in each sentence. Now, let us discuss the semantic roles in complex sentences. In this regard, Almanna (2018: 13) holds that complex sentences, unlike simple and compound sentences, can be analysed at different levels. To explain, let us consider the following example (for more examples, see Ibid.):

قرّر أخي أن يبيع سيّارته ويشتري سيّارة جديدة.

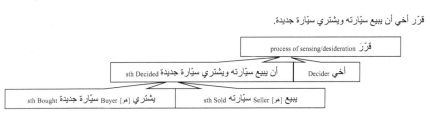

Semantic roles and flow of energy **89**

In the above sentence, two main verb-specific semantic roles can be identified, viz. Decider and sth Decided, as shown above. Inside the clause that fills a verb-specific semantic role of sth Decided (also known as the أَنْ-clause and complementizer clause), there are two clauses. They are:

- يبيع [هو = Seller] سيارته [sth Sold]
- يشتري [هو = Buyer] سيارة جديدة [sth Bought]

It is worth noting here that as it is not asserted that he sold his car and bought a new car, the scope of intention is greater than the extent of causation (for more details, see Chapter 7 of this book). Building on this, in order for the translators to produce a similar mental image, they need to pay undivided attention to the semantic role filled by each argument, rather than to the syntactic structure itself (Ibid.: 13). To make this point clear, the following example extracted from Mary Ali's text titled *Women's Liberation through Islam*, published on 24 June 2013 (www.islamreligion. com) and translated into Arabic by Al-'Abrī (2015: 31), can be discussed:

Islam grants women many rights in the home and in society.

Here, as can be noticed, the act of granting used to indicate something abstract and thus spiritual has been granted is employed by the writer where:

- *Islam* fills a semantic role of Source and Actor and a verb-specific semantic role of Granter,
- *women* fills a semantic role of Goal, Recipient and Beneficiary and a verb-specific semantic role of Grantee,
- *many rights* fills a semantic role of Theme and a verb-specific semantic role of sth Granted, and
- *in the home and in society* is just an adjunct that provides the reader with extra information.

This process is characterized by having a force-dynamic value where the Granter, i.e. Islam, enables the Grantee, i.e. women who have no rights or a limited number of rights, to have all these rights (for more details on force dynamics, see Chapter 7 of this book). Approached from a semiotic perspective, the act of granting in this context indicates the Granter's being-able-to-do (powerful) and the Grantee's being-able-not-to-do (dependent), not-being-able-to-do (powerless) and not-being-able-not-to-do (submissive). Having paid extra attention to the semantic roles filled by each argument, the translator has suggested the following translation:

منح الإسلام المرأة كثيرًا من الحقوق سواءً أكانت في المنزل أم في المجتمع.

As can be seen, there is an example of an intra-system shift, to use Catford's (1965) term. The translator has opted for a singular form – المرأة *woman* – in place of the plural form – *women* – used in the source text. The question that jumps into mind here: does that affect the mental image conjured up in our minds when we read both texts? The answer is 'No'. This is because the lexical term المرأة *woman* in such a context is characterized by multiplexity, that is, the quantity consists of more than one element, i.e. more than one woman, thus triggering a cognitive operation of unbounding (for more details on this cognitive operation, see Chapter 6 of this book). Cast in less technical terms, the lexical item المرأة *woman* here refers to all Muslim women.

Grammatical relations and semantic roles

Syntactically speaking, finite clauses (also called 'tensed clauses') normally consist of a noun phrase and a verb phrase. However, this does not exclude any other syntactic analyses; there are different syntactic analyses of any finite clause. In a statement like the following one:

My brother bought a new house some days ago.

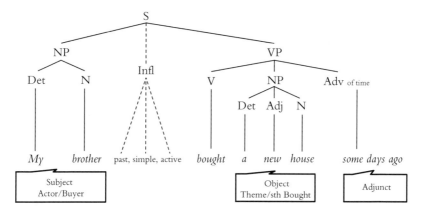

- the subject is *my brother*, filling a semantic role of Actor and a verb-specific semantic role of Buyer,
- the object is *a new house*, filling a semantic role of Theme and a verb-specific semantic role of sth Bought, and
- *some days ago* is just an adjunct as it is not an argument of the verb *to buy*, that is to say, it can be omitted.

In the actual act of translating from language *A* to language *B*, shall we pay attention to the grammatical relations, to semantic roles or to both? To address this question, the following examples extracted from different authentic sources and translated by professional translators can be discussed. To begin with, the following example extracted from a short story titled شعور الأسلاف *Ancestral Hair* by

Salwa Bakr (cited in and translated by Husni and Newman 2008: 210–211) can be discussed:

أنا يأكلني الخوف كلّ يوم ألف مرة. أخاف إلى درجة الرغبة في الصراخ أحياناً. أخاف أن أفقد وظيفتي...

I, on the other hand, am consumed by fear a thousand times every day. I am frightened I could scream sometimes. I am scared to lose my job and income . . .

In the above example, three mental processes are employed by the writer. Let us confine our discussion to the first process only, that is, يأكلني الخوف كلّ يوم ألف مرة. In this process used metaphorically, the subject is الخوف *fear* and the object is ني *me*, filling a semantic role of Experiencer. In the target text, as can be noticed, the subject is *I* (within a context of passivization that is not recognized in the source text) that fills a semantic role of Experiencer, and *fear* is just a noun phrase in the verb phrase of the clause. Despite these syntactic differences, a similar mental image has been produced in the target-language readers' minds. This is because the interaction between the text participants (be they explicit or implicit) in both texts is construed as unidirectional based on an asymmetrical action schema where the transfer of energy flows from an external participant filling a semantic role of Stimulus to *I* filling a semantic role of Experiencer. This clearly shows the importance of maintaining the semantic roles and energy transfer, if any, along with its directionality through translation.

To reinforce this, the following example taken from a short story titled ثلاث قصص ليست للنشر *Three Stories Not for Publishing* by 'Abdulsattar Nāṣir (translated by and cited in Almanna and Al-Rubai'i 2009: 14–15) can be considered:

وما أن أرجع نصف الأموال ثانية، حتى أعلن عن (نصر) كبير غامض، مات فيه عشرات الجنود، لكن السعادة كانت قد غمرت أهل المدينة كلهم... ذلك أن كل بيت فيها يردد سراً:
- الحمد لله لم يمت أحد منا...

Once he had restored the half of the treasury's revenues, he announced a mysterious and great 'victory' in which tens of soldiers had died. All the townsfolk were filled with happiness, each household repeating secretly, "Thanks be to God, none of us was killed".

As can be seen, in السعادة كانت قد غمرت أهل المدينة كلهم, the subject is السعادة *happiness* and the object is أهل المدينة *the townsfolk*. However, semantically speaking, the argument أهل المدينة *the townsfolk* fills a semantic role of Experiencer, and the tensed clause لم يمت أحد منهم *none of them was killed* is the source of happiness, thus filling a semantic role of Stimulus. Having given adequate consideration to these semantic roles assigned to each argument in the clause along with energy transfer (see below), the translators have managed to produce an accurate mental image. However, one may wonder here why this shift from active in the source text to passive in the target

92 Semantic roles and flow of energy

text! Had the translators opted for a rendering of the following kind – *happiness engulfed the townsfolk altogether* – in place of the one suggested above, they would have maintained not only the voice recruited in the source text but the semantic roles assigned to each argument as well.

Now, let us discuss the noun phrase *the knifeman* along with its equivalent in Arabic in the following example extracted from *BBC* (23 October 2017):

> *The knifeman reportedly sprayed a gas into the face of a security guard as he broke in.*
> وقالت تقارير إن الرجل الذي كان يحمل سكينا باغت حارس الأمن برش غاز في وجهه واقتحم مبنى الإذاعة لتنفيذ الهجوم.

As we may observe, the noun phrase *the knifeman* that fills a semantic role of Agent is the subject of the first finite clause *the knifeman reportedly sprayed a gas into the face of a security guard*. This noun phrase is changed to a noun phrase الرجل *the man* and a relative clause الذي كان يحمل سكيناً *who was carrying a knife*, thus changing the simple subject in English to a complex one in Arabic. However, despite the difference in the form of the subject, we still see in our mind's eye the man holding a knife in both versions.

To reinforce this point, let us look into the following sentence (discussed in Chapter 1) extracted from a passage given to level-one students (Dept. of Translation, University of Basrah) to be translated into English on one of their exams (2014):

> \# هدّد اللصُّ الرّجلَ بالسّكين.

As can be observed, by the effect of the preposition بـ used before the Instrument, i.e. السّكين *knife*, we have only one meaning in which the knife is with the thief – in our mind's eye, we see that the thief holds a knife, as can be shown in this picture:

This sentence has been translated by the majority of the students as:

The thief threatened the man with the knife.

Their suggested translation could mean either of the following meanings:

a   The thief threatened the man who was holding the knife, or
b   The thief used the knife to threaten the man.

Semantic roles and flow of energy **93**

Syntactically speaking, the difference between (a) and (b) is whether the prepositional phrase *with the knife* is grouped with the verb phrase *threatened the man* or just with the noun phrase *the thief*. Tree diagrams can be used here to show this difference.

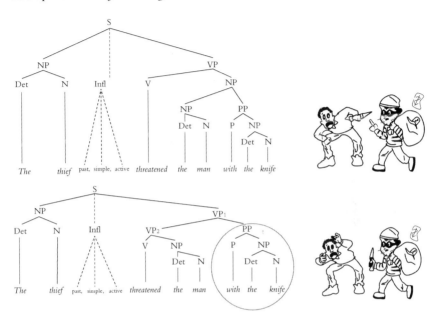

To avoid this syntactic ambiguity and reflect an accurate mental image, the translator can suggest a rendering where the knife filling a semantic role of Instrument is with the thief as in *With the knife, the thief threatened the man* or *The man was threatened by the thief with the knife*, to suggest only two.

To reinforce this point, let us discuss this sentence:

Visiting relatives can be boring.

This sentence has two interpretations. Therefore, the whole context has to be given serious consideration prior to making a judgement about the meaning of the sentence. In the first interpretation (see below), we talk about the relatives who visit their relatives in a process of being where *visiting relatives* is a noun phrase headed by the noun *relatives* with a participial adjective *visiting* as a modifier and *can be boring* is a verb phrase. Here, when the modal verb *can* is deleted, the main verb is *are*:

Visiting relatives are boring.

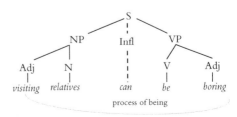

In the second interpretation, we talk about the act of visiting relatives. As such, here we have two processes: a process of doing and a process of being. *Visiting relatives*, which is a process of doing embedded in a process of being, is a non-finite clause functioning as a subject of the whole sentence, and *can be boring* is a verb phrase, as shown here:

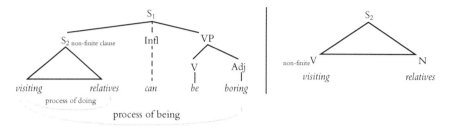

In this non-finite clause (S$_2$), the subject, which is said to be a non-overt nominal named PRO in the literature, is not specified but can be specified in similar sentences, such as:

Helping myself to the food was enjoyable. (the subject is 'I')

Washing your hands is the best way to remove bacteria. (the subject is 'You')

Let us go back to the second interpretation of our example, i.e. *visiting relatives can be boring*. When the modal verb *can* is deleted, the main verb is *is*:

Visiting relatives is boring.

To finish off this section, the following three examples extracted from a short story titled الشباك والساحة *The Window and the Courtyard* by Maḥmūd 'Abdulwahhāb (translated by and cited in Sadkhan and Pragnell 2012: 10–11) may be considered:

قال أحد المارة وهو يرفع رأسه:
— إنهم فوقنا يشربون الشاي ويقرأون الصحف.

In this example, a verbal process is utilized by the writer where:

- أحد المارة *one of the passers-by* is the Sayer filling the semantic role of Actor,
- قال *said* is the process of saying,
- وهو يرفع رأسه *while raising his head* is a circumstantial element manner/quality as it answers the question 'how' where there is no time interval between the act of saying and the act of raising his head, and
- إنهم فوقنا يشربون الشاي ويقرأون الصحف *they are above us drinking tea and reading newspapers* is the Verbiage of the process, that is, the content of what is said or indicated.

In the content of what is said, three processes are employed by the writer, viz.:

- a relational process إنهم فوقنا *they are above us* where the pronoun هم *they* fills a semantic role of Positioner, the implicit verb *to be* (*are*) is the process of being and فوقنا *above us*, which is an adverb of place, is treated as a participant (circumstantial element) in such a process,
- a material process in the form of an action process where the implicit pronoun هم *they* fills a semantic role of Actor/Agent, يشرب *to drink* is the process of doing and الشاي *tea* is the Goal filling a semantic role of Patient, i.e. Affected Participant, and
- a material process in the form of an action process where the implicit pronoun هم *they* fills a semantic role of Actor, يقرأ *to read* is the process of doing and الصحف *newspapers* is the Goal filling a semantic role of Theme.

It is worth noticing here that the two goals (note that the term 'goal' here is not used as a semantic role but as an optional participant in a process of doing; for more details, see the previous chapter in this book), that is, *tea* and *newspapers*, in the above material processes exist prior to the act of drinking and reading. As such, they are dispositive types of material process (Halliday1994: 111).

Reading or hearing the lexical items *to read* and *to drink* evokes in the mind of the hearer or reader different frame experiences, thus suggesting different scenarios. In each scenario, these acts are "associated with different scenes and frames along with different preconditions and (un)expected results" (Almanna 2016: 24). For some people, to read a newspaper requires a table, chair and the like, while for others it does not. Similarly, the act of drinking invokes different scenes and frames as nursing a drink is different from sipping it, slurping it, gulping it down, to mention but a few. Had the writer, for instance, opted for the use of the verb رشف *to sip* in place of شرب *to drink* or had he added a prepositional phrase, such as بجرعة واحدة *in/with one gulp*, he would have definitely created a different mental image in the mind of the hearer/reader.

Being fully aware of the processes along with the semantic roles assigned to each participant, time intervals and different frame experiences, the translators have produced an adequate translation, thus creating an accurate mental image.

> "*Above us they are drinking tea and reading newspapers*", said a passer-by raising his head.

Following is the second example (pp. 10–11):

صاحت امرأة من الداخل:
– هل أنت مسرور يا حبيبي؟

In this example, a verbal process is used. إمرأة *woman* is the Sayer filling a semantic role of Actor, صاح *to call out* is the act of saying in the past where the emphasis is put on the completion of the act of calling out, من الداخل *from inside* is a location circumstance construing the extent of the unfolding of the act of calling out in space and هل أنت مسرور؟ *Are you happy?* is the Verbiage of the process. The relationship

96 Semantic roles and flow of energy

between the in-text participants is sharply determined by the lexical item حبيبي lit. *my beloved* functioning as a vocative, which is frequently used in Arabic to show that the relationship between the interlocutors is strong and informal.

In هل أنت مسرور يا حبيبي؟, the argument أنت *you* fills a semantic role of Experiencer. The act of صاح invokes in the minds of the Omanis *crying*-frame while it invokes in the minds of the Iraqis, for instance, *calling out*-frame. Therefore, the translators, in addition to maintaining the semantic roles filled by each argument, need to reflect the different frames associated with the act of صاح to produce an accurate mental image.

Having given full consideration to the process of saying along with its participants and circumstances, semantic roles and different frames, the translators have suggested an accurate and adequate translation where a similar mental image has been produced.

> "*Are you happy, darling?*" called out a woman from inside.

In this dynamic scene (pp. 18–19), a number of semantic roles can be identified:

نطت قطة سوداء وسط الساحة، ونفضت قطرات المطر عن نفسها، ثم وثبت تحتمي بشجرة البمبر غير أنها سرعان ما خرجت ثانية إلى الطارمة، وكوّرت نفسها، بشكل ما، تحت سلّم قريب.

Here, a material process is used where قطة سوداء *a black cat* is the Actor of the process filling a semantic role of Theme (when we focus on the spatial relations) and Actor (when we focus on the act and its effect); نط *to leap* is the process of doing characterized by telicity, that is, it has a natural finishing point; and وسط الساحة *in the middle of the courtyard* is a location circumstance construing the extent of the unfolding of the process in space. In this process, unlike the endpoint, which is foregrounded in attention, the starting point is backgrounded in attention, but can be predicted as it is in our scope of prediction.

Another material process is used here where the letter ت attached to the verb (referring back to the black cat) is the Actor; نفض *to shake off* is the process of doing characterized by atelicity, that is, it has no natural finishing point, but rather the Actor has to stop shaking off the drops of rain for any reason; and قطرات المطر *the drops of*

Semantic roles and flow of energy 97

rain is the Goal of the process, filling a semantic role of Theme or Patient, depending on the degree of affectedness.

و | نفضت قطرات المطر عن نفسها

Another material process is used here where the letter ت attached to the verb (referring back to the black cat) fills a semantic role of Actor and Theme (as explained in the first process), وثب *to jump* is the process of doing characterized by telicity and تحتمي بشجرة البمبر *to take refuge under the gummy cherry tree* which is a non-finite clause of purpose introduced by an implicit لكي, لـ, etc. *to* is a cause circumstance construing the reason that motivated the black cat to jump. It is worth noticing that the rain is backgrounded in attention in this process, but it can be easily predicted as it is in our scope of attention.

ثم | وثبت تحتمي بشجرة البمبر

Another material process is used where the letter ت attached to the verb خرج (referring to the black cat) is the Actor of the process filling the semantic role of Theme and Actor (as explained in the first process), خرج *to go out* is the process of doing and إلى الطارمة *to the veranda* is a location circumstance construing the extent of the unfolding of the process in space filling a semantic role of Goal. The starting point of this process, which is mentioned in the previous clause, is the gummy cherry tree filling a semantic role of Source.

غير أنها سرعان ما | خرجت ثانية إلى الطارمة

98 Semantic roles and flow of energy

Here, a behavioural process is used where the letter ت attached to the verb كوّر referring back to the black cat is the Behaver of the process filling a semantic role of Actor, كوّر *to curl* is the process of behaving, بشكل ما *in a way* is a manner circumstance construing the way in which the process is actualized and presented and تحت سلّم قريب *under a nearby staircase* is a location circumstance construing the extent of the unfolding of the process in space.

و كوّرت نفسها، بشكل ما، تحت سلّم قريب

The event is narratively presented in motion in a specific period of time, and its beginning point and endpoint are at different locations in space. However, the act of raining which is mentioned indirectly نفضت قطرات المطر *it shook off the drops of rain* is backgrounded in attention. Similarly, the act of jumping to take refuge under a tree and the act of curling itself up under a staircase indicate the continuity of the act of raining in a specific period of time. All these acts are scanned sequentially, that is, they are located on the timeline. In an attempt to speed up the pace of events, the writer opts for certain connectors and adverbs, such as و *and* and سرعان ما *quickly*. Being fully aware of the processes utilized and the way in which they are presented, the translators have managed to produce accurate mental images.

> *A black cat leapt in the middle of the courtyard and shook off the drops of rain, and then jumped to take refuge under the gummy cherry tree. But, very soon, it came out again towards the veranda, curled itself up as best it could, under a nearby staircase.*

From the discussion of the above examples, it can be concluded that in order to create an accurate mental image, extra attention should be paid to the semantic roles assigned to each argument in a clause. However, this is not enough, as we sometimes maintain the semantic roles assigned to each argument, but we create slightly or completely different image(s) when we do not pay attention to issues such as plexity, time lapse, windowing of attention and the like (these issues will be discussed in detail in the next chapters).

Energy transfer and mental contact

Closely related to semantic roles is the flow of energy or energy transfer. To represent a certain socio-cultural experience, language users (be they writers or speakers) tend to employ certain processes (be it material, behavioural, mental, verbal, existential, etc.) and "determine in advance the action-chain schemas to represent the flow of energy between the participants in a given process whether it is bidirectional, that is, a reciprocal action schema, or unidirectional, that is, an asymmetrical action schema" (Almanna, forthcoming 2). To translate accurately, thus reflecting an accurate mental image, the translators need to give adequate consideration to the flow of energy between the participants. To illustrate, the following example adapted from Hans Küng's Book *Islam: Past, Present and Future* (cited in and translated by Al-Shuraīqī 2016: 27) may be given adequate consideration:

> *After independence, some Muslim states (Syria, Egypt, Turkey and Tunisia) nationalized the property of the waqf, and the land was redistributed.*

As can be observed, the writer opts for an active construction in the first finite clause *some Muslim states (Syria, Egypt, Turkey and Tunisia) nationalized the property of the waqf* and a passive construction in the second finite clause *the land was redistributed*. To begin with the first finite clause, the interaction between *some Muslim states* filling a semantic role of Agent and *the property of the waqf* filling a semantic role of Patient is construed as unidirectional based on an asymmetrical action schema where the transfer of energy flows from *some Muslim states* (Agent) to *the property of the waqf* (Patient). This active construction shifts the focus of attention towards the Agent (*some Muslim states*), rather than the Patient (*the property of the waqf*), although they are both foregrounded in attention. In the second finite clause, however, the writer opts for a passive construction *the land was redistributed* where the entity that undergoes the action, linguistically called the Patient, is *the land* placed before the verb and the entity that performs an action deliberately, linguistically called the Agent, is backgrounded in attention. This can be modelled as follows:

Unlike the active construction, this passive construction has its own schematic meaning which is independent of the meanings of its components. In this passive construction, the focus of attention is shifted towards the Patient and what happened to it (*the land*). The system of voice is classified by Halliday (1994: 169; also discussed in Bazzi 2009: 80) into two types, viz.:

- *middle,* where the Agent is backgrounded in attention, that is, it is not mentioned, and
- *effective,* where the Agent is foregrounded in attention either in an active construction (fronted) or a passive construction (delayed and grouped with the verb phrase).

Being fully aware of the differences between the active and passive constructions and their schematic meanings, on the one hand, and the differences between the middle and effective voice on the other hand, the translator has opted for:

وضعت بعض الدول الإسلامية ـ سوريا، ومصر، وتركيا، وتونس ـ ممتلكات الوقف تحت إدارة الحكومة الرسمية، وتمّ إعادة توزيع الأراضي.

To reflect greater empathy with the Patient rather than the Agent or due to the absence of certain information related to the Agent, to mention but a few reasons, the language user sometimes opts for an agentless passive construction. To explain, the following example was adapted from the *UNHCR* official website (27 June 2017), along with its official translation into Arabic:

After his nephew was shot trying to flee the old city of Mosul, Abu Taha was trapped.
بعد أن قُتل ابن أخيه وهو يحاول الفرار من مدينة الموصل القديمة، وقع أبو طه تحت الحصار.

Here, to promote the Patient (*Abu Taha's nephew*) and demote the Agent that is backgrounded in attention or to reflect their ignorance of the Agent's identity, the news editor and the translator have opted for a passive construction.

In the following example extracted from a short story titled يحدث كلّ صباح *This Happens Every Morning* by Maḥmūd 'Abdulwahhāb (translated by and cited in Sadkhan and Pragnell 2012: 58–59), the interaction between the two participants in the first finite clause يطيلان النظر إلى بعضهما is construed as bidirectional based on a reciprocal action schema where the flow of energy goes in both directions at the same time.

يطيلان النظر إلى بعضهما ثم يلتفت كلّ منهما، في آن واحد، إلى جهة مغايرة، هي تتشاغل بالنظر إلى الجهة المعاكسة، وهو يستأنف سيره متحاشيا معارفه من المارة.
They look at each other for some time and then both of them turn, at the same moment, in a different direction. She busies herself looking in the opposite direction, while he starts walking again, avoiding the passers-by that he knows.

By the effect of *each other*, the translators have managed to produce a reciprocal action schema where the two participants are actively involved. However, the act of looking in the target text is characterized by uniplexity (i.e. the quantity consists of only one element/look) while in the original text, by the effect of the verb يطيل, it consists of more than one element, that is, more than one look. Had the translators given this issue full consideration, they would have suggested a rendering such as *they kept looking at each other for some time*, thereby stretching the behavioural process over time (for more examples on uniplexity, as opposed to multiplexity, see Chapter 6 of this book).

We have seen from the discussion of the above examples that energy transfer should be given full consideration by the translators to produce an accurate mental image. However, not all clauses (be they finite or non-finite) can be analysed according to the flow of energy. To illustrate, the following example extracted from a short story titled قسمتي ونصيبي *Qismati and Nasibi* by Mahfouz (cited in and translated by Husni and Newman 2008: 118–119) can be considered:

وسعد قسمتي ونصيبي بالرفيقين الجديدين . . .
In the end, Qismati and Nasibi were pleased with their new playmates . . .

In this finite clause, a mental process is employed where قسمتي ونصيبي *Qismati and Nasibi* is the subject of the clause filling a semantic role of Experiencer and الرفيقان الجديدان *the new playmates* fills a semantic role of Stimulus. As can be observed, in this finite clause, there is no energy transfer as the subject does not act with volition, but rather 'the new playmates' is the source of happiness, thus filling a semantic role of Stimulus. In this regard, Evans and Green (2006: 604; emphasis in the original) who advocated the viewpoint adopted by Langacker (2002: 221) state:

> While the asymmetry in an action chain arises from the direction of the energy flow, the asymmetry in the EXPERIENCER-STIMULUS relation arises from the fact that the EXPERIENCER is conscious and sentient and is thus responsible for establishing mental 'contact' with the STIMULUS by creating a cognitive representation of the experience.

To finish this section, the following example extracted from a short story titled ليلة القهر *Night of Torment* by Laylā Al-'Uthmān (translated by and cited in Husni and Newman 260–1) and discussed in the previous chapter may be reconsidered:

سمعته ينشق نشقات متتالية سريعة كمن يبحث عن مصدر رائحة ما! أدركت أنه اكتشف رائحة جديدة.

As can be noticed, in these finite clauses:

- سمعته ينشق نشقات متتالية سريعة
- أدركت أنه اكتشف
- اكتشف رائحة جديدة

there is no energy transfer as the subjects do not act with volition. Rather, the subject of each clause establishes a mental contact with the source of sensory or emotional feeling in each clause. To put this differently, the Senser in these three processes of sensing, that is, *she*, *she* and *he*, fills a semantic role of Experiencer, and the source of sensory fills a semantic role of Percept. Being fully aware of the semantic roles along with the mental contact established between the Senser and the source of sensory, the translators have managed to produce accurate mental images when they have resorted to the following translation:

> ... *she heard him sniffing – fast, repetitive sniffs – like someone trying to ascertain the source of a particular smell. She realized that he had discovered a new smell.*

Key technical terms

- Accompaniment
- Affected Participant (Patient)
- Affecting Participant (Stimulus)
- Agent
- Argument
- Associate (Predicate)
- Benefactor (benefactive)
- Causer
- Energy transfer
- Experiencer
- Goal
- Instrument

- Location (locative)
- Mental contact
- Positioner
- Possessor
- Recipient
- Resultant (effect)
- Semantic case
- Semantic role
- Senser
- Source
- Theme
- Theta role

Exercises

Exercise 1: The following sentences are in the active form. Try to

    a identify the semantic roles assigned to each argument,
    b change them to passive,
    c identify the semantic roles assigned to each argument in the passive form, and
    d compare the semantic roles assigned to each argument in both versions.

> \# *My sister sent a great number of emails to the university some days ago.*
> \# *John bought a new house from his close friend last month.*
> \# *Yesterday, Sara borrowed some money from her brother.*
> \# *My mother gave me a gift three days ago.*
> \# *My father normally drinks a glass of water every hour.*

Exercise 2: For each of the semantic roles below, construct an English sentence. Then, translate your own sentences into Arabic without changing the semantic roles filled by each argument.

    1 Agent
    2 Patient

Semantic roles and flow of energy   103

3 Theme
4 Experiencer
5 Recipient
6 Instrument
7 Source
8 Goal
9 Stimulus
10 Possessor

Exercise 3: Put the following verbs in meaningful sentences. Then, design thematic role grids for each sentence, as in the first example.

1 to put: He [Who put it? =Actor] *put* his bag [What was put? = Theme] *on the chair* [where was it put? = Location].
2 to eat
3 to drink
4 to send
5 to walk
6 to buy
7 to write
8 to read
9 to play
10 to sleep

Exercise 4: Read the following short text taken from a short story titled قسمتي ونصيبي *Qismati and Nasibi* by Mahfouz (cited in and translated by Husni and Newman 2008: 138–139), along with its translation. Then, comment on the semantic roles in the second clause ولكن سرعان ما غشاه الفزع by identifying

a the subject and the object of the clause in both texts, and
b the semantic roles assigned to the two arguments occupied in the positions of the subject and object in both texts.

ST: بكى قسمتي أيضاً ولكن سرعان ما غشاه الفزع من الموت المزروع في جذعه، وتبادل الوالدان نظرة حائرة.

TT: *Qismati wept, but was suddenly gripped by fear and panic at having a corpse joined to his torso . . .*

Exercise 5: Identify the verb-specific semantic roles assigned to each argument in the following sentences. Then, compare each sentence along with its semantic roles with the three translations suggested.

أعطتها صديقتها قطعة نقدية.

TT1: # *Her friend gave her a coin.*
TT2: # *A coin was given to her by her friend.*
TT3: # *She received a coin from her friend.*

إِشْتَرَى أَخِي الأَكْبَرُ سَيَّارَةً جَدِيدَةً مِنْ جَارِهِ قَبْلَ أَيَّامٍ.

TT1: # My brother bought a new car from his neighbour some days ago.
TT2: # A new car was bought by my brother from his neighbour some days ago.
TT3: # My brother's neighbour sold a new car to my brother some days ago.

تَسَلَّمَتْ اِبْنَتِي الصَّغِيرَةُ يَوْمَ أَمْسِ بَعْضَ الهَدَايَا مِنْ أَصْدِقَائِهَا.

TT1: # My young daughter received some gifts from her friends yesterday.
TT2: # Some gifts were sent to my youngest daughter yesterday by her friends.
TT3: # My youngest daughter's friends sent her some gifts yesterday.

Exercise 6: Translate the following text extracted from an article titled *Decoding Daesh* by Alice Guthrie published on 19 February 2015 (www.freewordcentre.com) into English. Then, annotate your own translation, focusing on the semantic roles assigned to each argument in each clause.

Over the last few months, there has been a concerted effort by several senior global politicians to give a new name to the group known as ISIS, or Islamic State, IS or ISIL. That new name is 'Daesh'.

Exercise 7: The following text is extracted from a collection of poems titled إنَّ القَنَابِلَ لَمْ تُفْطِرِ الآنَ *Bombs Have Not Breakfasted Yet* by 'Adnān Al-Ṣā'īgh and translated into English by Kadhim and Sullivan (2013: 98–99; bilingual edn). Comment on the translation, paying extra attention to the semantic roles assigned to each argument.

In my childhood I had a doll   كَانَتْ لِي فِي طُفُولَتِي دُمْيَةٌ
Who was stolen before she learned to speak   سَرَقُوهَا قَبْلَ أَنْ تَتَعَلَّمَ النُّطْقَ
and play with me   وَتَلْعَبَ مَعِي
And I had a field of golden grains   وَكَانَ لِي فِي صِبَايَ حَقْلٌ ذَهَبِيٌّ مِنْ سَنَابِلَ
cut by water   قَطَعُوا عَنْهُ مَاءَ النَّهْرِ

Further reading

Almanna, A. (2016). *Semantics for Translation Students: Arabic-English-Arabic*. Oxford: Peter Lang.
———. (2018). *The Nuts and Bolts of Arabic-English Translation: An Introduction to Applied Contrastive Linguistics*. Newcastle upon Tyne, England: Cambridge Scholars Publishing.
Carter, R. (1998). *Vocabulary: Applied Linguistic Perspectives*. London/New York: Routledge.
Dixon, R. M. W. (1991). *A New Approach to English Grammar on Semantic Principles*. Oxford: Oxford University Press.
Dowty, D. (1991). "Thematic Proto-roles and Argument Selection", *Language*, Vol. 67, pp. 574–619.
Fillmore, C. (1968). "The Case for Case". In E. Bach and R. Harms (eds.), *Universals in Linguistic Theory*, pp. 1–81. New York: Holt, Reinhart and Winston.
Jackendoff, R. (1987). "The Status of Thematic Relations in Linguistic Theory", *Linguistic Inquiry*, Vol. 18, pp. 369–411.
———. (1990). *Semantic Structures*. Cambridge, MA: MIT Press.
Kearns, K. (2000/2011). *Semantics*. Basingstoke: Palgrave Macmillan.
Kreidler, C. W. (1998). *Introducing English Semantics*. London/New York: Routledge.

Löbner, S. (2002). *Understanding Semantics*. London: Hodder Education.
Saeed, J. I. (1997/2003). *Semantics*. Oxford: Blackwell Publishing.

References

Al-'Abrī, S. (2015). *Translating and Annotating Ideology-loaded Texts: 'Women Liberation Through Islam' and 'Thirty Facts About Islam' as Samples*. BA final Year Project. Oman: University of Nizwa.

Ali, M. (2013). *Women's Liberation Through Islam*. Accessed on 24 June 2015: <www.islam-religion.com>.

Almanna, A. (2016). *Semantics for Translation Students: Arabic-English-Arabic*. Oxford: Peter Lang.

———. (2018). *The Nuts and Bolts of Arabic-English Translation: An Introduction to Applied Contrastive Linguistics*. Newcastle upon Tyne, England: Cambridge Scholars Publishing.

———. (forthcoming 2). "Transitivity System as a Tool for Producing (In)accurate Mental Images Through Translation".

Almanna, A. and Al-Rubai'i, A. (2009; bilingual edn). *Modern Iraqi Short Stories: A Bilingual Reader*. London: Sayyab Books Ltd.

Al-Shuraīqī, M. (2016). *Translating Hans Küng's Book 'Islam: Past, Present and Future' and Annotating the Local Strategies Adopted*. BA final Year Project. Oman: University of Nizwa.

Bazzi, S. (2009). *Arab News and Conflict*. Amsterdam/Philadelphia, PA: John Benjamins Publishing Company.

Carter, R. (1998). *Vocabulary: Applied Linguistic Perspectives*. London/New York: Routledge.

Dixon, R. M. W. (1991). *A New Approach to English Grammar on Semantic Principles*. Oxford: Oxford University Press.

Dowty, D. (1991). "Thematic Proto-roles and Argument Selection", *Language*, Vol. 67, pp. 574–619.

Evans, V. and Green, M. (2006). *Cognitive Linguistics: An Introduction*. Edinburgh: Edinburgh University Press.

Fillmore, C. (1968). "The Case for Case". In E. Bach and R. Harms (eds.), *Universals in Linguistic Theory*, pp. 1–81. New York: Holt, Reinhart and Winston.

Guthrie, A. (2015). *Decoding Daesh*. <www.freewordcentre.com>

Halliday, M. A. K. (1994). *An Introduction to Functional Grammar* (2nd edn). London et al.: Arnold.

Husni, R. and Newman, D. (2008; bilingual edn). *Modern Arabic Short Stories: A Binigual Reader*. London: Saqi Books.

Jackendoff, R. (1987). "The Status of Thematic Relations in Linguistic Theory", *Linguistic Inquiry*, Vol. 18, pp. 369–411.

———. (1990). *Semantic Structures*. Cambridge, MA: MIT Press.

Kadhim, A. and Sullivan, D. (2013; bilingual edn). إن القنابل لم تفطر الآن *Bombs Have Not Breakfasted Yet*. London: Iraqi Cultural Centre.

Kearns, K. (2000/2011). *Semantics*. Basingstoke: Palgrave Macmillan.

Kreidler, C. W. (1998). *Introducing English Semantics*. London/New York: Routledge.

Langacker, R. W. (1991/2002). *Concept, Image, Symbol: The Cognitive Basis of Grammar* (2nd edn). Berlin: Mouton de Gruyter.

Löbner, S. (2002). *Understanding Semantics*. London: Hodder Education.

Sadkhan, R. and Pragnell, F. (2012). رائحة الشتاء *The Scent of Winter: A Bilingual Reader*. London: Sayyab Books Ltd.

Saeed, J. I. (1997/2003). *Semantics*. Oxford: Blackwell Publishing.

Thakur, D. (1999). *Linguistics Simplified: Semantics*. New Delhi: Bharati Bhawan.

6
IMAGING SYSTEMS I
The configurational system

The imaging systems (also known in the literature of cognitive linguistics as 'construal operations', 'schematic systems' and 'conceptualization processes') are given full consideration in this chapter and the next one. Following Talmy (2000), these imaging systems are divided into four types, namely (1) the configurational system, (2) the perspectival system, (3) the attentional system and (4) the force-dynamic system.

In the sense used by Talmy (Ibid.), these imaging systems work hand in hand to structure a given scene. The scene, then, is expressed via language. Therefore, when we translate from language *A* to language *B*, these imaging systems should be given full consideration to structure a similar scene.

This chapter confines itself to the first one in the imaging systems, that is, the configurational system, which refers to all forms of conceptualization of quantity or relations between quantities, in dimensions like TIME and SPACE. Seven schematic categories (i.e. 'plexity', 'state of dividedness', 'state of boundedness', 'degree of extension', 'pattern of distribution', 'axiality' and 'scene partitioning') that form the configurational system are considered in this chapter in a direct link with translation.

Plexity

Plexity refers to "a quantity's state of articulation into equivalent elements" (Talmy 2000: 48). When there is only one equivalent element, then the matter or action is characterized by uniplexity. However, when there is more than one equivalent element, then the matter or action is characterized by multiplexity. Cast in more technical terms, plexity in the domain of matter is closely related to the grammatical category 'number' (be it singular, dual or plural). However, in the domain of action, it is related to "the traditional aspectual distinction between 'semelfactive'

Imaging systems | **107**

and 'iterative' (the distinction between one and more than one instance of a point-like event, respectively)" (Evans and Green 2006: 2004). The act of smiling, for instance, in:

When I asked him about his name, he smiled.

is characterized by uniplexity as it encodes a semelfactive aspect. However, when it is drawn out over a period of time, as in:

When I asked him about his name, he kept smiling.

it is characterized by multiplexity as it encodes an iterative aspect. To make this point clear, the following example extracted from a short story titled بئر الآبار *The Well of Wells* by 'Aḥmad Khalaf (translated by and cited in Pragnell and Sadkhan 2011: 54–55) may be given full consideration:

قال أحد الفتيان: لم يكن أمامنا إلا دعوة جميع الناس لحفر الآبار واستخراج المياه من باطن الأرض. لم يكن أمام النساء والرجال والشيوخ والصبيان إلا أن يعملوا ليل نهار.
"We had no option, but to call people to dig wells and extract water from the depth of the earth", said a young man. Women, men, the elderly and the young had no choice but work day and night.

As can be noticed, the definite article *the* is used before the adjectives *elderly* and *young* in the target text to refer to two different groups of people. To put this differently, *the elderly* and *the young* are characterized by multiplexity, that is, the quantity consists of more than one element (more than an elderly man and more than a young man), thus triggering a cognitive operation of unbounding, as modelled below:

To reinforce this point, the following example adapted from a short story titled ثلاث قصص ليست للنشر *Three Stories Not for Publishing* by 'Abdulsattar Nāṣir (translated by and cited in Almanna and Al-Rubai'i 2009: 14–15) may be considered:

وزّع الملك نصف أمواله على الفقراء والمعدمين، وتوّج إمرأة أخرى على عرش المملكة، وعاش الناس في فرح وابتهاج ...

In the above example, the writer opts for the plural form to talk about two groups of people, namely الفقراء and المعدمين. They are characterized by multiplexity, that is, the quantity consists of more than one element, thus triggering a cognitive operation of unbounding. To reflect this in the target text, the translators have used the definite article *the* along with the adjectives *poor* and *needy*:

> . . . *the king distributed half of his wealth to the poor and the needy. He also crowned another queen to sit on the throne of the kingdom. The people lived in great happiness.*

In Arabic, plexity (be it uniplexity or multiplexity) can be expressed by المفعول المطلق 'cognate accusative' (for more details, see Almanna 2018: 26–27). To illustrate, the following example extracted from a short story titled علي الأحمر *Ali the Red* by Luʾaī Ḥamza ʿAbbas (translated by and cited in Pragnell and Sadkhan 2011: 84–85) may be discussed:

لم أفكر لحظتها بشيء بقدر ما فكرت بقنينة العرق التي يتركها جاسم مملوءة بالماء على حافة النافذة المفتوحة لتبرد، أمسكت بعنقها وأنتظرت حتى وصل أمام الغرفة، فصرخت صرخة سمعها سابع جار وهويت بها على هامته فانفجر دمه وشعرت برطوبته تبلل وجهي ورقبتي.
I could think of nothing but a wine bottle left by Jassem filled with water on the ledge of the open window to cool. I grabbed it by the neck and waited until he was in front of the room, I let out a cry that could be heard by the most distant neighbour and smashed it over his head; blood spurted out and I felt its wetness hitting my face and neck.

In the source text, by the effect of the cognate accusative صرخ صرخة, the act of screaming is characterized by uniplexity, that is, the quantity consists of only one element/scream. Being fully aware of this characteristic, the translators have opted for the phrasal verb *to let out* that collocates well with the noun *cry*, thus reflecting the act along with its uniplexity. Had the writer, for instance, opted for فراح يصرخ *he began screaming* where the act of screaming is characterized by multiplexity, that is, the quantity consists of more than one scream, he would have imposed on the scene different content specifications. As such, to create an accurate mental image, the quantity's state of articulation as to whether it consists of one element, two or more should be taken into account through translation.

To reinforce this point, the following example extracted from a short story titled شعور الأسلاف *Ancestral Hair* by Salwa Bakr (translated by and cited in Husni and Newman 2008: 212–213) may be considered:

جاءتني ذات مرة بعد منتصف الليل، تدق بابي دقاً متلاحقاً.
One day, she came to see me after midnight. She had been knocking on my door persistently.

In the above example, by virtue of the cognate accusative تدق دقاً, the act of knocking is characterized by multiplexity as its quantity consists of more than one element/knock. This has been reflected in the target text by the translators when resorting to the past perfect continuous tense *had been knocking* followed by an adverb of manner, i.e. *persistently*, thus stretching the material process over the timeline. In this partially bounded clause *she had been knocking on my door persistently*, the situation has

Imaging systems | **109**

a left-hand boundary but does not have a right-hand boundary (for more details on boundaries, see below). The act of knocking indicates that there is a material process, that is, رفعتْ يدها *she raised her hand*, which is backgrounded in attention in both texts. In these two processes, it is asserted that she raised her hand and knocked on the door; therefore, the extent of causation is greater than the scope of intention (these issues will be discussed in detail in Chapter 7).

State of boundedness

State of boundedness has two principal notions, namely 'bounded' and 'unbounded'. Countable nouns, such as *cars* or *dogs*, for example can be counted as they have bounded structures, that is, they have inherent boundaries. By contrast, non-countable noun, such as *sugar*, *tea* or *water*, cannot be counted as they do not have bounded structures.

Similarly, when we talk about an event, it could be bounded or unbounded, depending on the grammatical form adopted by the language user. In a bounded quantity, the initial portion of an event and its final portion are marked off either lexically or grammatically, as in:

Yesterday, he walked through the tunnel in 15 minutes.

In this aspectually bounded sentence, the adverbial *in 15 minutes* indicates the starting point and endpoint. Further, the motion path in the above example has a physical boundary coincident with the beginning point and endpoint of the tunnel. However, in a sentence of the following kind:

Yesterday, he had walked along the shore for half an hour.

the adverbial *for half an hour* indicates the starting point and endpoint, but the motion path has no physical boundary coincident with the beginning point and endpoint of the shore; therefore, it is unbounded. In this partially bounded sentence:

Until yesterday, no one had received his salary.

the situation has a right-hand boundary (till yesterday) but does not have a left-hand boundary, as modelled below:

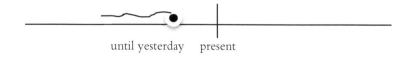

By contrast, in a partially bounded sentence like this:

I have been working in this company since 2016.

the situation has a left-hand boundary (2016) but does not have a right-hand boundary as the emphasis is placed on the period that started in the past (2016) and is seen as relevant to the present and its continuity, as shown below:

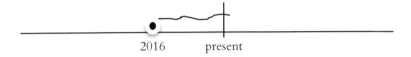

Now, let us discuss the state of boundedness in a direct link with the actual act of translating. Following is an example taken from a short story titled امرأة وحيدة *A Lonely Woman* by Zakariyyā Tāmir (translated by and cited in Husni and Newman 2008: 52–53):

انحنت عزيزة بإعياء، وكانت متعبة، وخجلة، والتقطت أوّل قطعة من ثيابها . . .

In the original text, the lexical item ثياب *clothes* is used in the plural from; therefore, it is characterized by multiplexity, that is, the quantity consists of more than one piece of clothing. By the effect of the phrase أوّل قطعة *the first piece*, it becomes bounded, thus triggering a cognitive operation of portion excerpting. Excerpting, as opposed to debounding, is a cognitive operation where "an unbounded mass entity is converted into a countable entity by virtue of a portion of the mass being 'excerpted'" (Evans 2007: 74). This has been reflected by the translators when resorting to the partitive *piece*:

Aziza bent down, weary and ashamed. She picked up a piece of her clothing.

Had the translators, for instance, suggested a rendering, such as:

Aziza bent down, weary and ashamed. She picked up her clothes.

the mental image would have been affected as the noun *clothes* is characterized here by multiplexity.

To reinforce this point, the following two examples extracted from a short story titled غيابات القلب: الغيابة الأولى الحليب *The Depths of the Heart: The First Deep: Milk* by 'Aḥmad Būzafūr (translated by and cited in Almanna and Hall 2015: 118–119) may be paid undivided attention:

اشتريت نصف لتر من الحليب، ليس عندي إبريق، غليت الحليب في (الكاصرونة)، حليته بالسكر، ثم صببته في فنجان القهوة. (لا كأس ولا صينية ولا صلصال)، نفخت على الحليب الساخن ليبرد.

I buy half a liter of milk, but I do not have a jug, so I boil it in a saucepan and sweeten it with sugar then pour it into the coffee cup (there is no cup, no tray, no clay) I blow on the hot milk to cool it.

Imaging systems | 111

By the effect of نصف لتر *half a liter*, the unbounded noun حليب *milk*, characterized by having no intervals or interruptions through the process of composition, becomes bounded, thus triggering a cognitive operation of portion excerpting. This has been taken into account by the translators when opting for *half a liter of milk*.

Following is the second example (pp. 116–117):

هو ذا (sic.) الطعم الأبيض الحلو يعود إليّ الآن بعد هذا العمر الطويل، وأنا الذي لم أذق الحليب منذ سن.السابعة، ولكنه يعود ممتزجا بطعم غريب: طعم كطعم التراب

The delicious white milk taste comes back to me now after all these years. I have not tasted it since I was seven years old, but it comes back mixed with a strange, earthy flavor ...

In the relative clause introduced by الذي ..., that is, لم أذق الحليب, by virtue of منذ سن السابعة *since I was seven years old*, the emphasis is placed on the whole period of not drinking milk that began in the past (at the age of seven) and is seen as relevant to the moment of speaking, as modelled below:

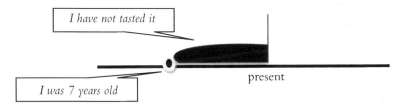

In this bounded clause لم أذق الحليب منذ سن السابعة, the situation has a left-hand boundary (since the age of seven) and a right-hand boundary (till now). This indicates that he did not taste milk at the age of eight, nor did he taste it a year ago. To emphasize the whole period since he was seven years old till now, the translators have opted for *have not tasted milk since I was seven years old*, thus producing a similar mental image.

To finish this section, the following example extracted from the *UNHCR* official website (27 June 2017), along with its official translation into Arabic, may be considered:

In Hammam Al Alil's reception centre, Abu Taha took a tiny bag from his wallet that contained barely a spoonful of powdered sugar. During the siege, he would mix a few specks of sugar with water in order to keep his children alive.

وفي مركز استقبال حمام العليل، أخرج أبو طه كيسا صغيرا من حقيبته يحتوي بالكاد على ملعقة من السكر. خلال الحصار، كان يخلط بضع حبيبات من السكر بالماء من أجل إبقاء أطفاله على قيد الحياة.

As can be observed, by virtue of the partitives and expressions of quantity *bag*, *spoonful* and *specks*, the unbounded noun *sugar* becomes bounded, thereby triggering a cognitive operation of portion excerpting. This has been reflected in Arabic by the effect of the partitives and expressions of quantity ملعقة, كيس and حبيبات, respectively.

112 Imaging systems I

State of dividedness

State of dividedness refers to the internal segmentations that a quantity has. When the quantity is characterized by having no intervals or interruptions through the process of composition, it is internally continuous, that is, it cannot be broken down into discrete matter. Otherwise, it is internally discrete, that is, it can be broken down into discrete matter. In the state of sleeping in a sentence of the following kind:

Last night, he slept very well.

the emphasis is placed on the completion of the state of sleeping in a specific period in the past. In this example, the state of sleeping is characterized by having no breaks or interruptions through the process of composition, thus it is internally continuous. However, the act of snoring in a sentence of this kind:

He kept snoring last night.

is characterized by having breaks or interruptions through the process of composition; therefore, it is internally discrete. To make this point clear, let us consider the lexical item شاي *tea* in the following example extracted from a short story titled علي الأحمر *Ali the Red* by Lu'aī Ḥamza 'Abbas (translated by and cited in Pragnell and Sadkhan 2011: 86–87):

وضع كوب الشاي أمامي ثم تساءل:
- هل تصدّق بأن الأرض تشتعل تحت أقدام العمّال؟

He put the cup of tea before me and inquired:
  - Do you believe that land burns under workers' feet?

In the above example, the lexical item شاي *tea* is discrete as it is conceptualized as consisting of distinct and unconnected elements through its composition, as modelled below:

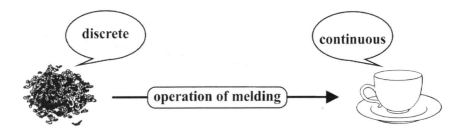

However, by the effect of the partitive كوب *cup*, it is characterized by boundedness as it triggers an operation of melding, whereby the unconnected elements of

Imaging systems | **113**

the original referent would be conceptualized as consisting of connected and continuous elements (for more details, see Talmy 2000: 56).

Disposition of a quantity

Disposition of a quantity is not a schematic category, but it is a term proposed by Talmy (2000) to cover these four areas:

- *domain* whether it is a matter or an action,
- *plexity* whether it is uniplex or multiplex,
- *state of boundedness* whether it is bounded, unbounded or partially bounded, and
- *state of dividedness* whether it is continuous or discrete.

For example, the non-countable noun *furniture* is a matter, multiplex, unbounded and discrete. However, the countable noun *chair* is a matter, uniplex, bounded and discrete. These four categories of attributes constitute the disposition of a quantity (Talmy 2000: 58). Building on this, any change in the disposition of the quantity through the nexus of translation will change the mental image. To explain, the following example quoted from *BBC* (23 October 2007) may be considered:

> *Tatyana Felgengauer is in a medically-induced coma in a Moscow hospital but her life is not said to be in danger.*
> ولا تزال المذيعة في غيبوبة منذ نقلها إلى مستشفى في موسكو. لكن التقارير الطبية تشير إلى أن حالتها مستقرة.

As the above example illustrates, the state of being in a medically induced coma in both versions is characterized by uniplexity, that is, the quantity consists of one element in addition to having no intervals or interruptions through the process of composition, that is, it is internally continuous. However, by the effect of منذ *since* employed in the Arabic version, it becomes partially bounded as it has a left-hand boundary (since she was admitted to hospital). To put this differently, in English, the state of being in a coma is approached from a distal perspective, thus being seen as a point on the timeline. However, in the Arabic version, it is drawn out over a period of time, as modelled below:

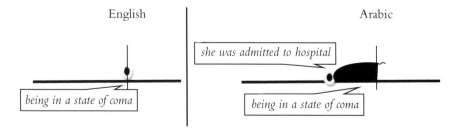

Had the news editors taken the disposition of the quantity, in particular the state of boundedness, into account, they would have suggested a rendering of this kind: *Tatyana Felgengauer has been in a medically-induced coma since she was admitted to hospital in Moscow.*

Degree of extension

Degree of extension has three principal member notions, viz. 'point of time', 'bounded extension' and 'unbounded extension'. By way of explanation, let us consider the following example adapted from a short story titled يوم في مدينة أخرى *A Day in Another City* by Maḥmūd 'Abdulwahhāb (translated by and cited in Sadkhan and Pragnell 2012: 22–23):

شقا طريقهما بين صف من الموائد الساج الصقيلة والمقاعد الجلدية وأصيص الأزهار الاصطناعية وعدد من الزبائن الموضوعين بعناية في مقاعدهم في غضون دقيقتين.
They made their way through a row of polished teak tables, leather seats, pots of artificial flowers, and a number of carefully-placed customers within two minutes.

Here, by virtue of في غضون دقيقتين *within two minutes* and ... بين صف من الموائد *through a row of tables ...,* the event referent of making one's way can be considered as an example of bounded extent. However, by the effect of a different grammatical form, such as *at 10 a.m.*, there will be an example of a point of time as it involves a cognitive operation of reduction, that is, it is approached from a distal perspective, thus being seen as a point on the timeline (Talmy 2000: 62). By contrast, when the language user employs a different grammatical form and content specifications, such as:

واستمرّا يشقان طريقهما بين صف من الأشجار في وسط الغابة.
They kept making their ways through a row of trees in the middle of the forest.

there will be an example of unbounded extent as it is approached from a proximal perspective, that is, it involves a cognitive operation of magnification (Ibid.). To reinforce this point, the following example taken from *BBC* (23 October 2017) may be given adequate consideration:

Just last month, another of its journalists, Yulia Latynina, left the country ...
وغادرت يوليا لاتينينا، الصحفية التي تعمل إيكو موسكوفي أيضا، البلاد الشهر الماضي ...

Here, although the act of leaving the country evokes in the mind of the hearer or reader different scenes and frames along with different preconditions and (un) expected results, it is approached in this example from a distal perspective, thus being seen as a point on the timeline. This has been reflected in both texts. Had an iterative expression, such as *three times*, been added by the news editor, the act of leaving would have drawn over a period of time in the past, thus being considered as an example of bounded extent.

Pattern of distribution

Pattern of distribution refers to the way in which the matter is distributed through SPACE and the action is distributed through TIME. To explain how an action, for instance, is distributed through TIME, let us consider the following verbs quoted from Talmy (2000: 63):

- *to die* under normal circumstances is one-way and non-resettable as one can die once; therefore, it is unacceptable to say *He kept dying* or *He died four times*.
- *to fall* is resettable for a one-way event characterized by its compatibility with iterative expressions, such as 'to keep + -ing', 'four times', etc. as in *He kept falling* or *He fell four times*.
- *to flash* means that a light, for example, keeps changing its state in a full-cycle form, that is, going from dark to light and back to dark and so on.
- *to breathe* refers to an iterated multiplexity of the component verbs *to inhale* and *to exhale*, and the verbs *to inhale* or *to exhale* refer to just one of these components. Repeating the cycle here is intrinsic part of the act of breathing.
- *to sleep* is characterized by its steady or unchanging state as it does not involve any internal change.
- *to widen* is gradient as it can be used with adverbs, such as *progressively*, as in *The river progressively widened*.

By way of illustration, let us discuss the verb *to die* in the following example taken from *Gulf Times* (www.gulf-times.com, 24 February 2017):

A Moroccan air force pilot died in May 2015 when his F-16 went down in Yemen.

Here, the verb *to die* is a non-resettable type of a one-way event as people die once. However, by the effect of certain grammatical forms and content specifications, a non-resettable type of a one-way event, such as *to die*, may become gradient, as in the following example extracted from a short story titled قسمتي ونصيبي *Qismati and Nasibi* by Mahfouz (translated by and cited in Husni and Newman 2008: 136–137):

هرولت إليه ست عنباية فأدركت أنه يحتضر فأخذته في حضنها وراحت تتلو الصمدية.
Sitt Anabaya rushed to him, realizing that he was dying. She held him close and started reciting the Surah of Fidelity.

In the target text, as can be observed, the non-resettable type of a one-way event *to die* becomes gradient by the effect of the grammatical form 'be + to die + ing'. This is an example of a shift in the pattern's distribution. Similarly, there will be a shift in the pattern's distribution of the internally discrete referent of verbs like *to breathe*, which is characterized by some partial degree of spontaneous melding when the language user opts for a structure of this kind: *He took a breath*, as in the following example quoted from a short story titled حكاية قديمة *An Old Tale* by Maḥmūd Jandārī (translated by and cited in Almanna and Al-Rubai'i 2009: 108–109):

خيل إليّ أن الحكاية قد انتهت، فتنفست بعمق وهمست بأن أقول شيئاً ولكنه منعني بإشارة يده. قال: غطت الجثة فوهة الحفرة في الأعلى وحجبت الضوء عني.

I thought that the story had ended. I took a deep breath and was about to say something when he stopped me with a wave of his hand. He continued, "The carcass covered the opening of the hollow and blocked out the light from me".

In the third finite clause تنفست بعمق, although the cognitive operation of actionalizing تنفست بعمق *I breathed deeply* has been reified to an object, that is, *breath* in *I took a deep breath*, the shift in the pattern's distribution of the internally discrete referent of the verb *to breathe* has been given full consideration by the translators.

Axiality

Axiality refers to the way in which a quantity of SPACE or TIME is structured according to a directed axis. By way of explanation, the following example extracted from a short story titled شعور الأسلاف *Ancestral Hair* by Salwa Bakr (cited in and translated by Husni and Newman 2008: 212–213) can be considered:

وجدتها أمامي في حالة إعياء واضحة، قالت إنها متعبة جداً.

I found her standing in front of me, looking very faint. She said she felt very sick.

In the above example, a verbal process is utilized where the implicit pronoun هي *she* is the Sayer, قالت *to say* in the past is the process of saying and إنها متعبة جداً *she felt very sick* is the Verbiage of the process. In the Verbiage, a HEALTH axis is employed by the writer and reflected by the translators. Here, on the HEALTH axis, the adjective *well* is the endpoint while the adjective *sick* is the reminder of the axis (Talmy 2000: 64). This clearly explains why it is acceptable, for example, to say *she's slightly sick*, *she's sick*, *she's very sick*, *she's is almost well* and *she's well*, as modelled below:

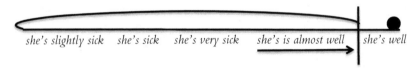

Scene partitioning

Scene partitioning refers to the conceptualization of the whole scene along with its parts and participants. While parts in this category refer to the arguments along with the verb, participants refer to the personation type, which can be:

- 'monadic' when there is only one participant, or
- 'dyadic' when there are two participants.

In a sentence of the following kind:

She sent me an email.

the act of sending is characterized by having a dyadic personation type, that is, *sender* and *receiver* and a four-part scene partitioning where there are three arguments, viz.:

- the pronoun *she*, filling a semantic role of Actor and a verb-specific semantic role of Sender,
- the pronoun *me*, filling a semantic role of Recipient and a verb-specific semantic role of Receiver, and
- the lexical item *email*, filling the semantic role of Theme and a verb-specific semantic role of sth Sent (for more details on semantic roles, see Chapter 5 of this book).

To make this point clear, the following example extracted from a short story titled مطر أسود *Black Rain* by Salām 'Abūd (translated by and cited in Pragnell and Sadkhan 2011: 94–95) can be given full consideration:

فُتح الباب فظهرت أمه بملابسها البيضاء. توقفت أمامه مندهشة، مترددة، خائفة . . .

The door opened and his mother appeared, dressed in white. She stood before him amazed, hesitant and frightened . . .

Here, we have three explicit processes, viz.:

- فُتح الباب
- ظهرت أمه بملابسها البيضاء
- توقفت أمامه مندهشة، مترددة، خائفة

To begin with the first material process, فتح *to open* is the process of doing, and الباب *the door* is the goal, that is, the affected participant. The act of opening in this context is characterized by having a monadic personation type and a two-part scene partitioning where there is one argument, viz. *the door* filling the semantic role of Theme and a verb-specific semantic role of sth Opened. This material process invokes in our mind an implicit process of being, that is, the door was closed.

In the second material process, أمه *his mother* is the Actor, ظهرت *to appear* is a material process where the emphasis is placed on the completion of the action and بملابسها البيضاء is a manner circumstance/quality construing the way in which the process is actualized and presented, answering the question 'with what'. The act of appearing is characterized by having a monadic personation type and a two-part scene partitioning, that is, *she* and the verb *to appear*.

The third process is a behavioural process: the implicit pronoun هي *she* is the Behaver filling the semantic role of Actor; توقفت *to stop* is the process of behaving characterized by atelicity, that is, having no natural finishing point, but the person has to stop for a particular reason; أمامه *in front of him* is a location circumstance construing the extent of the unfolding of the process in space; and مندهشة، مترددة، خائفة

amazed, hesitant and frightened is a manner circumstance construing the way in which the process is actualized and presented. The act of standing in this context is characterized by having a monadic personation type and a two-part scene partitioning.

To conclude this section, the following example adapted from a short story titled غيابات القلب: الغياب الأولى الحليب *The Depths of the Heart: The First Deep: Milk* by 'Aḥmad Būzafūr (translated by and cited in Almanna and Hall 2015: 118–119) may be reconsidered here as it was discussed in this chapter from a different perspective:

اشتريت نصف لتر من الحليب، غليت الحليب في (الكاصرونة)، حليته بالسكر، ثم صببته في فنجان القهوة. . . . نفخت على الحليب الساخن ليبرد

As can be observed, a number of material processes are employed by the writer, as in:

A process of doing The act of buying is characterized by having a monadic personation type and a three-part scene partitioning where there are two arguments, viz. the implicit pronoun *I* filling a semantic role of Actor/Agent and نصف لتر من الحليب *half a liter of milk* filling a semantic role of Theme.	اشتريت نصف لتر من الحليب
A process of doing The act of boiling is characterized by having a monadic personation type and a four-part scene partitioning where there are three arguments, viz. the implicit pronoun *I* filling a semantic role of Actor/Agent, الحليب *milk* filling a semantic role of Affected Participant and في الكارصونة *in a saucepan* filling a semantic role of Instrument.	، غليت الحليب في (الكارصونة)
A process of doing The act of sweetening is characterized by having a monadic personation type and a four-part scene partitioning where there are three arguments, viz. the implicit pronoun *I* filling a semantic role of Actor/Agent, the explicit pronoun ـه – *it* – referring back to the milk – filling a semantic role of Affected Participant and السكّر *sugar* filling a semantic role of Integrant.	، حليته بالسكر
A process of doing The act of pouring is characterized by having a monadic personation type and a four-part scene partitioning where there are three arguments, viz. the implicit pronoun *I* filling a semantic role of Actor/Agent, the explicit pronoun ـه – *it* – referring back to the milk – filling a semantic role of Theme, and في فنجان قهوة *in a coffee cup* filling a semantic role of Location.	ثم صببته في فنجان القهوة

A process of doing The act of blowing is characterized by having a monadic personation type and a four-part scene partitioning where there are three arguments, viz. the implicit pronoun *I* filling a semantic role of Actor/Agent, الحليب الساخن *the hot milk* filling a semantic role of Affected Participant and ليبرد *to be cool* is a cause circumstance construing the reason why the process is actualized, thus answering the question 'for what purpose'.	، نفخت على الحليب الساخن ليبرد.

These processes, along with their participants, circumstances and characteristics, have been given full consideration by the translators, as in:

> *I buy half a liter of milk, but I do not have a jug, so I boil it in a saucepan and sweeten it with sugar then pour it into the coffee cup ... I blow on the hot milk to cool it.*

Key technical terms

- Axiality
- Boundedness
- Bounding
- Configurational system
- Debounding
- Degree of extension
- Dividedness
- Excerpting
- Magnification
- Multiplexity
- Pattern of distribution
- Plexity
- Reduction
- Scene partitioning
- Unboundedness
- Unbounding
- Uniplexity

Exercises

> *Exercise 1:* The following example is adapted from a short story titled علي الأحمر *Ali the Red* by Lu'aī Ḥamza 'Abbas (translated by and cited in Pragnell and Sadkhan 2011: 88–89). Identify the cognitive operation triggered by virtue of بعض *some* used before the countable noun قصاصات *slips*.

In forensic medicine, they gave me his belongings before I saw his body. They included an identity card, driving license and some slips of paper ... in a plastic transparent bag ...	في الطب العدلي سلموني أشياءه قبل أن أرى جثته، كانت بطاقة الأحوال الشخصية وإجازة السياقة وبعض قصاصات الورق . . . في كيس نايلون شفاف . . .

> *Exercise 2:* The following example is extracted from the *UNHCR* official website (27 June 2017), along with its official translation into Arabic. Identify whether the material process فرت *she escaped* is bounded, unbounded

or partially bounded. Then, compare its state of boundedness with its equivalent in English.

| *After a rock struck her home in the Shifa neighbourhood, Maysa Muhammed, 47, escaped through the rubble.* | فرت ميساء محمد (47) من تحت الأنقاض بعد سقوط صاروخ على منزلها في حي الشفاء. |

Exercise 3: Identify the scene partitioning in both versions in the following example extracted from *BBC* (23 October 2017).

| *One of the broadcaster's security guards was injured as the knifeman was being overpowered.* | أصيب في الهجوم أحد حراس الأمن في الإذاعة أثناء محاولة السيطرة على المسلح. |

Exercise 4: The following text is extracted from a short story titled الزر *The Button* by 'Alī Muḥammad Al-Ja'kī (translated by and cited in Zagood and Pragnell 2017: 2–3). Identify the disposition of the quantity of غرفة, فنادق ساعات and دفء ألفة along with their equivalents.

| *I first met him in a cold room in a third class hotel that had everything but cleanliness and warmth. A kind of camaraderie linked us in spite of the few hours that we spent together* | جمعتني به غرفة باردة في أحد فنادق الدرجة الثالثة الموحية بكل شيء، إلا النظافة والدفء ربط بيننا نوع من الألفة رغم الساعات القليلة التي قضيناها معا. |

Exercise 5: Translate the following text extracted from an essay titled *5 Things About Life in Japan You Probably Don't Know* (cited in Al-Sā'dī 2015: 1–2). Then, annotate your own translation by focusing on the configurational system.

Life in Japan can be challenging, but also absolutely amazing and wonderful. Having spent two years in the country of the rising sun as a kid I still remember quite a lot of things that kept me thrilled and amazed. Here are five things about the Japanese lifestyle that you should know before moving in or traveling to this wonderful country!
One of the first things you notice in Japan – trash cans are impossible to find at public places! Yet, there's no litter on the streets either and by no means you should become the one who leaves it! So, what are you expected to do with your bento pack? Put it in your bag and carry it home like all the Japanese people do.

Further reading

Croft, W. (1998). "Mental Representations", *Cognitive Linguistics*, Vol. 9 (2), pp. 151–174.
Evans, V. and Green, M. (2006). *Cognitive Linguistics: An Introduction*. Edinburgh: Edinburgh University Press.

Johnson, M. (1987). *The Body in the Mind: The Bodily Basis of Meaning, Imagination, and Reason*. Chicago: University of Chicago Press.

Langacker, R. ([1991] 2002). *Concept, Image, Symbol: The Cognitive Basis of Grammar* (2nd edn). Berlin: Mouton de Gruyter.

Langacker, R. (2008). *Cognitive Grammar: A Basic Introduction*. Oxford: Oxford University Press.

Lee, D. (2001). *Cognitive Linguistics: An Introduction*. Oxford: Oxford University Press.

Leech, G. and Svartvik, J. (2002). *A Communicative Grammar of English*. London: Longman.

Talmy, L. (2000). *Toward a Cognitive Semantics: Vol. 1: Concept Structuring Systems*. Cambridge: MIT Press.

Taylor, J. (2002). *Cognitive Grammar*. Oxford: Oxford University Press.

Ungerer, H. and Friedrich, S. (1996). *An Introduction to Cognitive Linguistics*. London: Longman.

References

Almanna, A. and Al-Rubai'i, A. (2009; bilingual edn). *Modern Iraqi Short Stories: A Bilingual Reader*. London: Sayyab Books Ltd.

Almanna, A. and Hall, M. (2015; bilingual edn). *Moroccan Short Stories: A Bilingual Reader*. München: Lincom Europa Academic Publishers.

Al-Sāʿdī, S. (2015). *5 Things About Life in Japan You Probably Don't Know*. MA Translation Project. Oman: University of Nizwa.

Croft, W. (1998). "Mental Representations", *Cognitive Linguistics*, Vol. 9 (2), pp. 151–174.

Evans, V. (2007). *A Glossary of Cognitive Linguistics*. Edinburgh: Edinburgh University Press.

Evans, V. and Green, M. (2006). *Cognitive Linguistics: An Introduction*. Edinburgh: Edinburgh University Press.

Husni, R. and Newman, D. (2008; bilingual edn). *Modern Arabic Short Stories: A Binigual Reader*. London: Saqi Books.

Johnson, M. (1987). *The Body in the Mind: The Bodily Basis of Meaning, Imagination, and Reason*. Chicago: University of Chicago Press.

Langacker, R. ([1991] 2002). *Concept, Image, Symbol: The Cognitive Basis of Grammar* (2nd edn). Berlin: Mouton de Gruyter.

Langacker, R. (2008). *Cognitive Grammar: A Basic Introduction*. Oxford: Oxford University Press.

Lee, D. (2001). *Cognitive Linguistics: An Introduction*. Oxford: Oxford University Press.

Leech, G. and Svartvik, J. (2002). *A Communicative Grammar of English*. London: Longman.

Pragnell, F. and Sadkhan, R. (2011). *Ten Stories from Iraq: A Bilingual Reader*. London: Sayyab Books Ltd.

Sadkhan, R. and Pragnell, F. (2012). رائحة الشتاء *The Scent of Winter: A Bilingual Reader*. London: Sayyab Books Ltd.

Talmy, L. (2000). *Toward a Cognitive Semantics: Vol. 1: Concept Structuring Systems*. Cambridge: MIT Press.

Taylor, J. (2002). *Cognitive Grammar*. Oxford: Oxford University Press.

Ungerer, H. and Friedrich, S. (1996). *An Introduction to Cognitive Linguistics*. London: Longman.

Zagood, M. and Pragnell, F. (2017; bilingual edn). أموت كلّ يوم *I Die Every Day*. München: Lincom Europa Academic Publishers.

7

IMAGING SYSTEMS II

Attention, perspective and force dynamics

The previous chapter looked into the configurational system and how it structures matter and action in SPACE or TIME. Seven schematic categories, namely 'plexity', 'state of dividedness', 'state of boundedness', 'degree of extension', 'pattern of distribution', 'axiality' and 'scene partitioning' were discussed in a direct link with the actual act of translating. In this chapter, special attention is paid to the other imaging systems, namely the attentional system, perceptival system and force-dynamic system.

Distribution of attention

This system is concerned with the distribution of attention over the aspects of the scene along with its participants. In this imaging system, serious consideration is given to issues such as foregrounding versus backgrounding in attention, figure-ground organization, windowing of attention, scope of attention, profile selection, strength of attention whether it is placed on the scope of intention or extent of causation and so on. To make a start, this example written for the purposes of this course can be discussed:

My brother travelled to London two days ago to visit his family.

In this example, an open path with windowing over the final portion (indicated by the white oval at the end of the path) is employed by the writer. This is because the emphasis in this example is placed on the completion of the act of travelling in a specific period in the past. In this example, only the final portion of the path (Goal) is foregrounded in attention while the initial portion

(Source) and medial portion (Path) are backgrounded in attention, as modelled below:

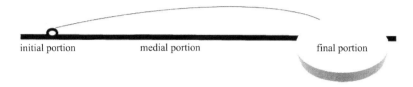

Further, in the non-finite clause of purpose *to visit his family* introduced by *to*, the scope of intention is greater than the extent of causation as it is not asserted that he visited his family. Had the writer, for instance, opted for a different grammatical form such as وزار عائلته and *he visited his family*, s/he would have imposed different content specifications on the scene where the extent of causation becomes greater than the scope of intention. To reflect a similar mental image in which an open path with windowing over the final portion is used and the scope of intention is greater than the extent of causation, one may suggest a rendering of the following kind:

سافرَ أخي قبل يومين إلى لندن ليزور عائلته.

To make this point clear, the following example extracted from a short story titled صفحة من كتاب الموتى *Excerpt from The Book of The Dead* by Ibrāhīm Al-Faqīh (translated by and cited in Husni and Newman 2008: 86–87) may be considered:

عاد من جديد يسترق النظر إليها عله يجد شيئاً في ملامحها يضيء ما اعتراه من حيرة وذهول.
Once again he glanced over at her, and noticed something in her features that shed light on what had baffled him.

By the effect of عله, the scope of intention is greater than the extent of causation. However, in the target text, the translators have imposed different specifications on the scene when they have opted for the additive connector *and*, thereby emphasizing the completion of the act of noticing at a specific point in the past. Had they given the scope of intention and extent of causation adequate consideration, they would have suggested a rendering of the following kind:

Once again he glanced over at her in an attempt to notice something in her features that shed light on what had baffled him.

In the following example extracted from a short story titled ما يشبه القصة – التاج *Story-Like: The Crown* by Wārid Badir as-Sālim (cited in Almanna and Al-Rubai'i 2009: 142–143), a closed path is utilized by the writer:

أحضرتُ كرسي المطبخ الوحيد وغطيته بإزار شتوي من الصوف كثير الألوان المبهجة.

Here, in the first finite clause أحضرتُ كرسي المطبخ الوحيد *I brought the only kitchen chair*, a closed path with windowing over the final portion is employed by the writer. To elaborate, in this closed path while the final portion of the path is foregrounded in attention, the initial portion and medial portion of the path are backgrounded in attention. Had the writer opted for different grammatical forms, such as ذهبتُ إلى المطبخ لأحضر الكرسي *I went to the kitchen to bring the chair*, he would have imposed different content specifications on the scene where the scope of intention in the non-finite clause of purpose introduced by لـ *to*, i.e. لأحضر كرسياً *to bring a chair*, is greater than the extent of causation. Giving full consideration to the distribution of attention, the translator may suggest a rendering of this kind:

I brought the only kitchen chair and put a lovely colourful wintery wool wrap over it.

Now, let us compare the closed path used in the previous example with this closed path in the following example extracted from a short story titled شعور الأسلاف *Ancestral Hair* by Salwa Bakr (translated by and cited in Husni and Newman 2008: 212–213):

سحبتها بسرعة لداخل شقتي، مددتها على سريري، جريت إلى المطبخ لأناولها شربة ماء طلبتها لأن ريقها جاف . . .
I quickly drew her into my flat and made her lie down on my bed. I ran to the kitchen to get her some water, as she complained her mouth was dry.

Here, the readers are invited to place their perspective points somewhere inside the depicted house, looking at the main participants in the scene. In the third finite clause جريت إلى المطبخ *I ran to the kitchen*, a closed path with gapping over the final portion is utilized in the source text جريت إلى المطبخ and reflected in the target text *I ran to the kitchen*. . . .

To make this point clear, the following example extracted from a short story titled لا تنسني *Forget Me Not* by Ibrāhīm 'Aḥmad (translated by and cited in Pragnell and Sadkhan 2011: 174–175) may be considered:

بعد سنوات من قلقي على فائزة وصلتني رسالة أخذت طريقا طويلا ومتعرجا ولم يكن في المظروف الصغير سوى بضعة كلمات . . .
After years of worrying about Faiza, I received a letter which had taken a long and roundabout route. There was nothing in the small envelope but a few words . . .

In this excerpt, the interaction between the Actor/Sender (*Faiza*) backgrounded in attention, but it can be easily predicted as it is in our scope of prediction and the Receiver (*me*) filling the semantic role of the Recipient is construed as uni-directional based on an asymmetrical action schema where the transfer of energy flows from *Faiza* (Actor/Sender) to *me* (Recipient). This active construction shifts the focus of attention towards the Recipient, rather than the Actor. In this scene, an open path with gapping over the initial portion, where a series of acts, such as writing the letter, putting it in an envelope, going to the post office, paying for it, coming back home, etc. are backgrounded in attention, is employed by the writer and reflected in the target text, as modelled below:

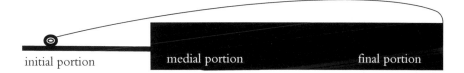

Croft and Cruse (2004: 47) state that in a particular semantic domain, the process of selecting a particular lexical item will draw our attention to the different elements that the lexical item has in the domain. To illustrate, the following example adapted from a short story titled القطار الصاعد إلى بغداد *The Train Heading up to Baghdad* by Maḥmūd ʿAbdulwahhāb (translated by and cited in Pragnell and Sadkhan 2011: 11) may be given full consideration:

تخضخض القطارُ فأسرعتُ إلى العربة وأخذتُ مكاني إلى جانب رجلٍ . . .

The train gave a jolt, and so I hurried to the carriage and took my seat beside a man . . .

As can be observed, in the original text, three finite clauses are employed. Each lexical item selected in these clauses has a certain profile in a certain semantic frame. To explain, let us confine our discussion to the verb تخضخض. In this domain, the verb تخضخض is profiled in a frame where it contrasts with verbs, such as تحرّك *to move*, اهتزّ *to shake* and so on. The verb تخضخض is characterized by an iterated multiplexity, to use Talmy's (2000) terminology, as it refers to a series of delicate movements forward and backward, and the verb *to move* refers to just one of these components (for more details on plexity, see the previous chapter in this book). In the first finite clause تخضخض القطار, a cognitive operation of actionalizing is used by the writer. However, it has been reified to an object, that is, *jolt* by the translators, thereby imposing different content specifications and semantic effect. By contrast, in the third finite clause أخذت مكاني إلى جانب رجل *I took my seat beside a man*, a cognitive operation of reification is used in place of the cognitive operation of actionalizing, that is, جلست *I sat*. This has been reflected by the translators when they have opted for *I took my seat*.

In أسرعت إلى العربة وأخذت مكاني إلى جانب رجل, an open path with gapping over the medial portion is employed by the writer and reflected by the translators, as modelled below:

As can be seen, an implicit material process, that is, مشيت داخل العربة *I walked inside the carriage*, is backgrounded in attention. This has been reflected by the translators when they have backgrounded it in the target text, thus creating a similar mental image in their readers' minds.

In the rest of this section, some politically loaded excerpts taken from various sources can be discussed. The following example taken from *BBC* (25 March 2015) can be examined:

> *Since the air campaign began, at least 39 civilians, including six children under the age of 10, have been killed, Yemen health minister officials say.*

In this example, a verbal process is employed by *BBC* where *Yemen health minister officials* is the Sayer, *to say* is the process of saying and *since the air campaign began, at least 39 civilians, including six children under the age of 10, have been killed* is the Verbiage of the process (for more details on transitivity processes, see Chapter 4 of this book). In the Verbiage of the process, a material process is unitized where the Actor of the process filling a semantic role of Agent and a verb-specific semantic role of Killer is backgrounded in attention, thus laying more emphasis on the Patient. This fits hand in glove with Kress and Hodge's (1979: 181) view that "the passive allows the actor to remain unspecified and, if specified, to occur at the end of the clause and thus carry unmarked information focus". Further, by the effect of the present perfect used in the material process, the act of killing is drawn out over a period of time that started in the past and is seen as relevant to the present. As such, the act of killing in this example is characterized by boundedness as it has a left-hand boundary (*since the air campaign began*) and a right-hand boundary (*till now*). To reflect a similar mental image in the mind of the target reader, these issues, in addition to the other issues discussed throughout this book, should be given adequate consideration by the translator. In such a politically loaded text, any change in the imaging systems will not only change the mental image but will promote a different narrative. In this context, Hart (2014: 172) rightly comments that "language has the facility to recruit alternative image schemas to conceptualize the same (kind of) situation and thus impose upon it alternative, ideologically vested, construals". Had the news editor opted for a structure of the following kind:

> # *Since the air campaign began, Saudi-led forces have killed at least 39 civilians, including six children under the age of 10, Yemen health minister officials say.*

s/he would have recruited alternative image schemas where *Saudi-led forces*, filling a semantic role of Agent, i.e. the source of energy, is foregrounded in attention.

To observe how removing the Agent of the action can twist the message to varying degrees, the following headlines published by *BBC* (23 October 2017) may be considered:

Russian radio presenter Felgengauer [Patient] *stabbed in neck*

((إسرائيلي)) [Agent] يطعن مذيعة روسية [Patient] داخل غرفة أخبار محطة إذاعة إيكو موسكوفي

As can be noticed, by virtue of the passive voice employed by *BBC* in its English version, the focus of attention is shifted towards *Felgengauer*, i.e. the stabbed person filling a semantic role of Patient/Affected Participant. By doing so, the focus of attention is shifted away from the Agent. In the Arabic version, however, by the effect of the active voice, the focus of attention is shifted towards the Agent. To create distance and hostility towards the Agent, the Arabic version resorts to explicitly naming the nationality of the Agent, thus touching the feelings of the Arabs. With respect to informativeness, the English version provides us with less information as we no longer have an indication about the Agent in the act of stabbing.

To conclude this section, the following example taken from *BBC* (1 November 2017) can be considered:

غادر بوجديمون [Actor] إسبانيا [Source] إلى بلجيكا [Goal] مع بعض الوزراء السابقين [Company].

Here, an open path with gapping over the final portion is employed by *BBC* in its Arabic version. To elaborate, in Arabic, a process of doing is utilized where:

- بوجديمون *Puigdemont* is the Actor of the process,
- إسبانيا *Spain* is the starting point, i.e. Source,
- بلجيكا *Belgium* is the endpoint, i.e. Goal, and
- مع بعض الوزراء السابقين *with some former ministers* is an accompaniment circumstance filling a semantic role of Company, thus indicating they also left Spain to Belgium with the Actor.

Here, although Puigdemont and some former ministers left Spain to Belgium together, more emphasis is put on the Actor, i.e. Puigdemont, as it is brought to the focal subject position.

In its English version, *BBC* opts for a process of being:

Mr Puigdemont is in Belgium with several former ministers.

The open path with gapping over the final portion employed by *BBC* in its Arabic version is lost when a process of being is resorted to by *BBC* in its English version. The emphasis in the English version is placed on the state of being in Belgium (Location) with several former ministers (Company), thus creating a completely different mental image.

Force dynamics

Unlike the other imaging systems, which focus on visual perception (Evans and Green 2006: 199), force dynamics as an imaging system "derives from kinaesthesia (our bodily experience of muscular effort or motion) and somesthesia (our bodily experience of sensations such as pressure and pain)" (Ibid.). Force dynamics deals with the forces that each and every element in the scene may exert on another element. These forces that an element may exert on another can be in the form of force, resistance to force, overcoming of such resistance, blockage to the exertion of force and the removal of such blockage (for more details, see Talmy 2000). When force-dynamic patterns are discussed, two entities, i.e. agonist and antagonist, are assumed (Talmy 2000: 413; also discussed in Evans 2007: 83). While the agonist refers to "the entity that receives focal attention", the antagonist refers to "the entity that opposes the agonist, either overcoming the force of the agonist or failing to overcome it" (Evans 2007: 83). To explain, the following excerpt taken from a short story titled الطوفان *The Flood* by 'Alī Muḥammad Al-Ja'kī (translated by and cited in Zagood and Pragnell 2017: 60–61) may be considered:

تابعت سيرها [she=Agonist] رغم التعب [Antagonist] الذي ألم بها وخدر قدميها.

In this example, the use of the conjunction رغم *in spite of* indicates that the force of the agonist هي *she* is not overcome by the force of the antagonist التعب *tiredness*. As such, this does not entail any causality. This has been reflected in the target text when the translators have opted for *in spite of*:

> *She walks on in spite of the tiredness which hurts her and numbs her feet.*

Had the writer resorted to different grammatical forms and content specifications, such as:

لم تتابع سيرها [she=Agonist] بسبب التعب [Antagonist] الذي ألم بها وخدر قدميها.

he would have imposed on the scene a different force-dynamic pattern where the force of the agonist هي *she* is overcome by the force of the antagonist التعب *tiredness*, thus entailing causality.

In the following example extracted from *BBC* (1 November 2017), by virtue of the conjunction *despite*, the force of the agonist (Carles Puigdemont), who decided to hold an independence referendum, is not overcome by the force of the antagonist (Madrid's opposition and the Constitutional Court), who tried to prevent him from doing so.

> *Carles Puigdemont triggered a crisis in Spain by holding an independence referendum in early October in the semi-autonomous region despite Madrid's opposition and the Constitutional Court declaring the vote illegal.*

Imaging systems II   **129**

In its Arabic version, *BBC* opts for deleting the non-finite clause of concession introduced by *despite*, thus changing the force-dynamic pattern.

وتسبب بوجديمون بأزمة في إسبانيا منذ أن أجرت حكومة إقليم كتالونيا الانفصالية استفتاء للاستقلال يوم 1 أكتوبر/تشرين الأول، كما أعلنت المحكمة الدستورية بأن التصويت على الاستفتاء غير قانوني.

To make this point clear, these two examples taken from a novella titled الفراشة والزهرة *The Butterfly and the Blossom* by Zahrā' Nāṣir (translated by and cited in Fred Pragnell 2017: 32–33) may be considered:

لمّا أحسّتْ أنّ أجنحتها لا تقوى على حملِها بسبب الجوع، توَقَّفتْ عند النهر وجلستْ على صخرةٍ صغيرةٍ قُربَ ضفته. نظرتْ إلى النهرِ وبدأتْ تُناجيه:
When she felt that her wings could not carry her because of hunger, she stopped at the river and sat on a small rock near the bank. She looked at the river and started talking to it.

In this example, the force of the agonist الفراشة *the butterfly* that tends to fly is overcome by the force of the antagonist الجوع *hunger*, thus entailing causality توقفت عند النهر *she stopped at the river*.

Following is the second example (pp. 36–37):

ازداد ألم جُروح السلحفاة فتوقفت عن الكلام لحظات ثمّ استطردت قائلة: ((خرجتُ من تحت الشجيرات كنتُ عَطشى أردتُ الوصولَ إلى النهرِ لكني فقدتُ وعيي هُنا ولم أصحُ إلا في الصَباح)).
The pain increased, so she stopped talking for a few moments and added: "I got out from under the bushes. I was thirsty and wanted to get to the river but I fainted here. I did not wake up until morning".

In the original text, the finite clause توقفت عن الكلام لحظات is an expected result of the finite clause ازداد ألم جروح السلحفاة. Here, there is a shift from a force-neutral selection process to a force-dynamic pressure. This force-dynamic framework enables us to capture the causing (the pain increased) of the expected result (she stopped talking for a few moments). Having analysed the text and figured out the relationship between the two clauses, the translator has opted for *so*, thus maintaining the relationship intact. Further, the act of getting out of the bushes is an expected result of the state of being thirsty. The relationship between the two clauses is introduced without any conjunction in both texts.

The following example extracted from *BBC* (1 November 2017) depicts a scene in which a shift from a force-neutral selection process to a force-dynamic pressure is opted for in both versions.

Spain's high court has summoned sacked Catalan leader Carles Puigdemont and 13 other members of his dismissed government to appear later this week.
استدعت المحكمة العليا في إسبانيا رئيس إقليم كتالونيا المقال كارلس بوجديمون ومسؤولين آخرين لاستجوابهم هذا الأسبوع بشأن التهم الموجهة إليهم.

The verb *to summon* employed by *BBC* in its English version is not force-dynamically neutral, but rather it is characterized in such a context by having a force-dynamic value of forcing the sacked Catalan leader, Carles Puigdemont, and 13 other members of his dismissed government – who tend, in normal circumstances, not to go to the high court – to go to the high court. In this example, we are informed by our encyclopaedic knowledge that the sacked Catalan leader along with the other members of his dismissed government are forced to go to the high court by a legal force. This has been reflected in Arabic when the verb استدعى *to summon* is used by *BBC* in its Arabic version.

The Actor and some former ministers in the following example, which is discussed in the previous section (*BBC*, 1 November 2017) are not forced to leave the country by a legal force or a physical force, but it is most likely they are forced by a political force, i.e. to be heard by the rest of the world.

وغادر بوجديمون إسبانيا إلى بلجيكا مع بعض الوزراء السابقين. وأكد رئيس إقليم كتالونيا المقال أنه جاء إلى بروكسل من أجل إسماع صوته في الاتحاد الأوروبي، ولا يعتزم طلب اللجوء السياسي.

However, the force that obliges Mr Puigdemont along with some former ministers to leave the country is not specified by *BBC* in its English version, thus changing the force-dynamic pattern:

> *Mr Puigdemont is in Belgium with several former ministers. He earlier said he was not there to seek asylum.*

At times, the participant's desire to act or not to act in a certain way is overcome by a social force. To illustrate, the following example extracted from a short story titled الشجرة المقدسة *The Sacred Tree* by Muḥammad Al-Zafzāf (translated by and cited in Husni and Newman 2008: 60–61) may be considered:

فكرّت أن عليها أن تعول أطفالها الثلاثة، الذين تركهم لها الزوج وانتقل إلى حيث سيذهبون جميعا. وعادت تقول للتي بجوارها:
– الحكومة تعرف ما تفعل، لو لم تجد مصلحة في قطع تلك الشجرة لما فعلت ذلك.

In the above example, a mental process is employed by the writer where the implicit pronoun هي *she* is the Senser, فكرّت *to think* in the past is the process of sensing, and أن-clause is a complementizer clause. In عليها أن تعول أطفالها الثلاثة, the modalized preposition along with the implicit verb كان in كان عليها *she had to* encodes a scene where the Senser's social obligation forced her to stop criticizing the government. So, here the use of the modalized preposition على *have to* indicates that she stopped criticizing the government only as the result of much arm-twisting. As a result, there is a shift from a force-neutral selection process to a force-dynamic pressure. This force-dynamic framework enables us, as readers/viewers, to capture the

Imaging systems II   **131**

causing (her social obligation) of the result (stopped criticizing the government). Being fully aware of the function of the modalized preposition على, the translators have opted for *had to*, thus reflecting such a social obligation in the past:

> She thought about the three children she had to feed after her husband had passed away. She continued talking to the woman next to her: "The government know what they're doing. They wouldn't cut the tree if there wasn't a good reason".

Now, let us line up these *BBC* news items on the same topic (3 November 2017) to discuss the force-dynamic patterns in both versions:

> Other reports said the Syrian forces and allies were clearing the last pockets of resistance from IS.
> أشارت تقارير أخرى إلى أن القوات الحكومية والقوات الموالية لها كانا في مهمة لتمشيط دير الزور بحثاً عن ما أسموه ((آخر جيوب المقاومة لتنظيم الدولة)).

As can be seen, *BBC* in both versions opts for the past continuous tense *were clearing* and كانا في مهمة لتمشيط, thus emphasizing (1) the continuity of the Syrian forces in forcing the IS who tend to stay in the city to leave the city and (2) the continuity of the IS to resist the Syrian forces. This indicates that at the moment of publishing these reports, the IS forces were still resisting the Syrian forces and its allies who were trying to overcome such resistance. Had the news editors in *BBC* employed different grammatical forms (e.g. *had cleared* and قد مشطّت), as in:

> \# Other reports said the Syrian forces and allies had cleared the last pockets of resistance from IS.
> # أشارت تقارير أخرى إلى أن القوات الحكومية والقوات الموالية لها قد مشطّت آخر جيوب المقاومة لتنظيم الدولة.

they would have depicted a scene where the IS's resistance to the Syrian forces and its allies is overcome, thus entailing causality.

To finish off this section, the following example extracted from a short story titled مطر أسود *Black Rain* by Salām 'Abūd (translated by and cited in Pragnell and Sadkhan 2011: 94–95) can be discussed here:

> جرته من كفه الوسخة التعبة باتجاه باحة الدار. سار خلفها طائعا مثل طفل كبير، جارا رجليه الحافيتين المتورمتين، وهو ينظر بدهشة الى وجوده المحيّر في هذا المكان شديد الألفة، شديد الغرابة.

> *She pulled him by his weary, dirty hand to the courtyard of the house. He followed her like an obedient big child, dragging his bare, swollen feet, as he looked with astonishment at his helpless presence in this place so familiar, yet so strange.*

132 Imaging systems II

Here, two main material processes followed by a behavioural process without any time gap among these processes are employed by the writer. Let us confine our discussion to the first two finite clauses only:

- جرته من كفه الوسخة التعبة باتجاه باحة الدار *she pulled him by his dirty, weary hand to the courtyard of the house* is a material process characterized by having a force-dynamic value of forcing the Affected Participant that tends towards rest to move. In this process, the implicit pronoun هي *she* is the Actor filling a semantic role of Agent, جرّ *to pull* is the process of doing, the pronoun ـه *him* is the Goal of the process, من كفه الوسخة التعبة *by his dirty, weary hand* is a manner circumstance and باتجاه باحة الدار *toward the courtyard of the house* is a location circumstance construing the extent of the unfolding of the process in space. It is worth noting that the act of pulling in such a context, in addition to giving rise to another implicit material process, that is, they walked along the courtyard of the house, is characterized by atelicity, i.e. having no natural finishing point; rather, the Actor has to decide to stop walking for any reason.

- سار خلفها طائعا مثل طفل كبير، جارا رجليه الحافيتين المتورمتين *he walked behind her like an obedient big child, dragging his bare, swollen feet* is a material process where the implicit pronoun هو *he* is the Actor, سار *to walk* is the process of doing where the emphasis is put on the completion of the act of walking characterized by atelicity and duration, طائعا *obediently* is a manner circumstance, مثل طفل كبير *like a big child* is a manner circumstance and جاراً رجليه الحافيتين المتورمتين *dragging his bare swollen feet* is another manner circumstance describing both his feet and his way of walking. Approached from another perspective, the act of walking in this context, along with the manner circumstances, indicates the Actor's being-able-not-to-do (dependency), not-being-able-to-do (powerlessness) and not-being-able-not-to-do (submission).

Deployment of perspective

This system is concerned with how people fix their mind's eye to look out upon a scene and its participants. Four schematic categories can be given consideration here. They are 'location', 'distance', 'mode' and 'direction' (cf. Talmy 1988, 2000; Evans and Green 2006; Evans 2007, among others). In what follows, these four schematic categories are discussed with reference to the actual work of the translators.

Location

Location as a schematic category refers to the position of the perspective point from which the scene at hand is viewed; it is viewed from outside by adopting an 'exterior perspective point' or from inside by adopting an 'interior perspective point' (Talmy 2000: 69). This perspective point can be identified by relying on certain grammatical forms and content specifications. By way of illustration, the following example extracted from a short story titled إمرأة وحيدة *A Lonely Woman* by Zakariyyā Tāmir (translated by and cited in Husni and Newman 2008: 48–49) can be given full consideration:

ازدادت رائحة البخور وتكاثفت، وراحت عزيزة تتنفس بصوت مسموع. وهتف الشيخ سعيد فجأة:
((تعالوا تعالوا يا مباركين تعالوا)).

Here, the reader as an observer or viewer is induced by the writer to locate his/her perspective point somewhere inside the depicted room, thus smelling the incense, looking at Aziza while breathing and hearing the Sheikh shouting. The position of the perspective point from which the scene is viewed is taken into account by the translators when they have resorted to:

> *The smell of incense grew much stronger. Aziza started to breathe loudly. Sheikh Said shouted: "Come, blessed ones, come!"*

To elaborate, the following excerpt taken from a short story titled الشباك والساحة *The Window and the Courtyard* by Maḥmūd 'Abdulwahhāb (translated by and cited in Sadkhan and Pragnell 2012: 20–21) can be examined:

وقف الفرّاش عند باب الصف ثم استدار نحو نهاية الطارمة ورفع رأسه إلى السماء، ولما وجدها متجهمة بالغيوم عاد بعجلة يغلق أبواب الصفوف وينصرف. أغلق الفرّاش أبواب الصفوف ومسح يده ووجهه بيشماغه وأسرع، بحيوية خارج الساحة.

Here, the readers are invited to place their perspective point somewhere in the schoolyard, looking at the janitor while standing at the door of the classroom, turning towards the end of the veranda, raising his head towards the sky, coming back, closing the classrooms, wiping his hand and face with his handkerchief and dashing out into the courtyard. To put this differently, the readers are induced here to zoom in on the janitor by adopting a proximal perspective, which results in a more restricted frame where other details of the school and its yard are backgrounded in attention. Being fully aware of the position of the perspective point from which the scene is viewed, the translators have managed to induce their readers to locate their perspective point somewhere in the schoolyard, thus producing similar images:

> *The janitor stood at the door of the classroom, and then turned towards the end of the veranda, raised his head towards the sky, and on finding it overcast, he came back immediately to close the classroom doors and left. The janitor closed the classrooms, wiped his hands and face with his handkerchief and dashed out into the courtyard.*

Distance

Distance as a schematic category refers to the distance of the elements of the scene at hand from the reader as a viewer. When there is a great distance between the readers, as observers, and the scene depicted, then a distal perspective is adopted by the readers, thus resulting in a less restricted frame (Evans and Green 2006; Evans 2007). By contrast, when there is no distance between the readers and the scene at hand, then a proximal perspective is adopted by the readers, thereby resulting in a more restricted frame. By the effect of certain grammatical forms or content specifications, the readers as viewers can adopt a distal perspective, medial perspective or proximal perspective. By way of exemplification, the following example discussed above can be reconsidered:

ازدادت رائحة البخور وتكاثفت، وراحت عزيزة تتنفس بصوت مسموع. وهتف الشيخ سعيد فجأة: ((تعالوا تعالوا يا مباركين تعالوا)).

Here, the readers are invited by the writer to adopt a proximal perspective in order to be able to see and smell the incense and hear Aziza breathing. However, to hear the Sheikh shouting, there is no need for the readers to adopt a proximal perspective as they can hear him shouting by adopting a medial or even a distal perspective. The distance between the scene depicted and the reader has been given full consideration by the translators when they have suggested this rendering:

> *The smell of incense grew much stronger. Aziza started to breathe loudly. Sheikh Said shouted: "Come, blessed ones, come!"*

Closely related to distance is 'zooming', as a construal operation, where the distance of the reader's camera, so to speak, from the depicted scene is given extra attention. To explain, the following excerpt taken from a short story titled قسمتي ونصيبي *Qismati and Nasibi* by Mahfouz (translated by and cited in Husni and Newman 2008: 114–115) can be examined:

واختلفت بقدرة قادر صورتاهما، فبدا قسمتي عميق السمرة رقيق الملامح عسليّ العينين، أما نصيبي فكان ذا بشرة قمحية وعينين سوداوين وأنف ينذر بالضخامة.

Here, a cognitive operation of zooming in is utilized by the writer where he invites his readers to zoom in on Qsmiti's face and then zoom in on Nasibi's, thus resulting in a more restricted frame. By virtue of the transition marker أما *as for*, the readers are encouraged to swing their camera around the scene in a horizontal axis, moving from one participant to another. Being fully aware of this, the translators have resorted to *while*, thus reflecting a similar restricted frame:

> *Thank God, they had different features; Qsmati had a deep brown complexion, with soft lineaments and hazel eyes, while Nasibi had a white complexion with black eyes and a large nose.*

Mode

Perspectival mode as a schematic category refers to whether the perspective point is in motion or not. According to Talmy (2000: 70), when the perspective point is in motion, then it is in a sequential mode; otherwise, it is in a synoptic mode. To be considered as a synoptic mode, the reader/viewer needs to adopt a distal perspective. By contrast, when a proximal perspective is adopted by the reader/viewer, then the perspective mode is sequential (Ibid.). It is worth noting that whether the perspective point is in motion or not is related to (1) the distance, i.e. whether the perspective is distal or proximal and (2) the scope of attention whether it is global or local (Ibid.). To illustrate this, the following example taken from a short story titled وجه *Face* by 'Abdulḥamīd Al-Gharbāwī (translated by and cited in Almanna and Hall 2015: 32–33) may be considered:

- ماذا كنت تكتب؟
  فاجأني السؤال.
- كنت أكتب شيئاً.
- لكنك كنت مرة مرة، تتفحصني بنظراتك ثم تنزل على الورقة كتابة.

Here, by the effect of the adverbial iteration مرة مرة *from time to time*, the perspective point is in motion, thus triggering a cognitive operation of sequentializing, to borrow Talmy's (2000) term. This has been reflected by the translators when they have suggested the following translation:

- *"What were you writing?"*
  I was taken aback by the question.
- *"I was writing something that concerns me".*
- *"But, from time to time you were examining me".*

Had the writer resorted to ولكنك منذ أن جلسنا هنا وأنت تتفحصني بنظراتك *but you have been examining me since we sat here*, he would have invited his readers to adopt a distal perspective in which the perspective point is not in motion, thereby triggering a cognitive operation of synopticizing, to use Talmy's (2000) term. This synoptic mode is triggered off by the presence of منذ *since* that induces the readers of this example to look into, in addition to the continuity of the act of examining (progressive aspect), the whole period that started in the past and is seen as relevant to the present as one unit without breaks (perfect aspect).

To reinforce this point, these two examples from a short story titled القطار الصاعد إلى بغداد *The Train Heading up to Baghdad* by Maḥmūd 'Abdulwahhāb (translated by and cited in Pragnell and Sadkhan 2011: 10–12) may be considered:

أدرت رأسي صوب المدينة فاعترضت نظري برية معتمة تلمع فيها من بعيد مصابيح مستوحشة كئيبة تمدّ ظلالها المريضة في شوارع البصرة الفوارة بالناس.

Here, by the presence of من بعيد *far off*, the readers are induced to adopt a distal perspective in which a cognitive operation of synopticizing is triggered. Being fully aware of this, the translators have suggested the following translation in which the perspectival system is given full consideration.

> *I turned my head towards the city, and a dark open space came into my view, in which there shone far off, dreary, gloomy street lamps that stretched their sickly shadows along the streets of Basra bustling with people.*

Had the writer, for instance, inserted an expression of quantity, such as عدد من *a number of*, before the noun مصابيح *lights*, a cognitive operation of sequentializing would have been triggered, on the one hand; on the other hand, the distance between the depicted object, i.e. مصابيح *lights*, and the reader as a viewer would have been reduced.

Following is the second example (pp. 22–23):

عمل لأكثر من خمس وعشرين سنة موظفاً ضئيل الراتب لا ينتظر في حياته جديداً إلا الموت.

By the effect of لأكثر من خمس وعشرين سنة *for more than 25 years*, the readers are invited to adopt a distal perspective, thus looking into the whole period that started in the past and is seen as relevant to another point in the past as one unit without interruptions. By doing so, a cognitive operation of synopticizing is triggered. This has been given serious consideration by the translators when they have opted for a past perfect:

> *He had worked for more than 25 years as a low-paid functionary waiting for nothing new in his life but death.*

Direction

Direction as a schematic category refers to the direction from which the depicted scene is viewed. It is closely related to attention (Evans 2007: 55). According to Talmy (2000; also discussed in Evans and Green 2006; Evans 2007), there are two directions, viz. 'prospective' and 'retrospective'. By way of clarification, the following example adapted from the *UNHCR* official website (27 June 2017), along with its official translation into Arabic, may be considered:

> *After his nephew was shot trying to flee the old city of Mosul, Abu Taha was trapped.*

Here, by the effect of the grammatical form *After . . . , Abu Taha . . .* opted for by the news editor, the readers are induced to place their perspective point at *his nephew was shot trying to flee the old city of Mosul* and from which a line of viewing in a prospective direction moves towards *Abu Taha was trapped*. The direction from which the scene is viewed is taken into account when it is translated into Arabic as:

بعد أن قُتل ابن أخيه وهو يحاول الفرار من مدينة الموصل القديمة، وقع أبو طه تحت الحصار.

Had the translator or trans-editor opted for a rendering of the following kind:

وقع أبو طه تحت الحصار بعد أن قُتل ابن أخيه وهو يحاول الفرار من مدينته الموصل القديمة.

s/he would have changed the direction from which the scene is viewed. Here, the readers are invited to place their perspective on the finite clause وقع أبو طه تحت الحصار *Abu Taha was trapped* and from which a line of viewing in a retrospective direction goes back to ... قُتل ابن أخيه وهو يحاول الفرار *his nephew was shot trying to flee*....

To make this point clear, the following example extracted from a short story titled امرأة مختلفة *A Different Woman* by Maḥmūd ʿAbdulwahhāb (translated by and cited in Sadkhan and Pragnell 2012: 62–63) may be considered:

دخل الصالة الليلية بعد ان انهى مكالمته التلفونية مع زوجته، ودسّ بامتعاض داخل جيبه، الورقة المجعدة التي كان يعصرها بين اصابعه.

In this excerpt, by virtue of بعد أن *after*, the readers are encouraged to place their perspective point at the finite clause دخل الصالة الليلية *he entered the evening bar* and from which a line of viewing in a retrospective direction goes back to انهى مكالمته التلفونية مع زوجته *he finished a call with his wife* and دسّ بامتعاض داخل جيبه الورقة *he stuffed the piece of paper into his pocket in annoyance*. The direction from which the scene is viewed is given full consideration by the translators when they have suggested the following translation:

> *He came into the evening bar after he had finished telephoning his wife, and in annoyance stuffed into his pocket the crumpled piece of paper he had been pressing between his fingers.*

Had the translators resorted to a rendering of this kind:

> # *He had finished telephoning his wife, and in annoyance stuffed into his pocket the crumpled piece of paper he had been pressing between his fingers before he came into the evening bar.*

they would have changed the direction from which the events are viewed. Here, the readers are induced to locate their perspective point at *he had finished telephoning his wife*... and from which a line of viewing in a prospective direction goes forward to the act of entering the evening bar.

Imaging systems II

Key technical terms

- Actionalizing operations
- Agonist
- Antagonist
- Closed path
- Distal perspective
- Distribution of attention
- Extent of causation
- Figure-ground organization
- Force dynamics
- Medial perspective
- Open path
- Perspectival system
- Prospective direction
- Proximal perspective
- Reification
- Retrospective direction
- Scope of intention
- Sequential mode
- Synoptic mode
- Zooming
- Windowing of attention

Exercises

Exercise 1: Read the following sentences to identify whether they have a force-dynamic value or not. Then, translate them into English, paying extra attention to force-dynamic patterns.

\# لم تتمكَّن من حضور اجتماعٍ إلا بسبب مرضها المفاجئ.

\# لأنه كان بأمسِ الحاجة إلى المال، اضطُرَّ إلى بيع بيتهِ الذي ورثه من أبيه.

\# على الرغم من رغبتها الكبيرة في الذهاب معه إلى الحفلة، إلا أنها قررت أن تبقى في البيت لترعى أمه المريضة.

\# على الرغم من أنه لا يحبُّ العيش في المدن الكبيرة، إلا إنه انتقل مؤخراً للعمل في مدينة كبيرة لأسباب عائلية.

\# أمهلتِ المحكمة بعض الوزراء مهلة أقصاها ثلاثة أيام لدفع وديعة تقدر بسبعين ألف دولار أمريكي لتغطية تكاليف الالتزامات القانونية.

Exercise 2: Read the following example extracted from the *UNHCR* official website (27 June 2017), along with its official translation into Arabic to identify:

a whether the scene is construed as having a force-dynamic value or not,
b whether an open path or a closed path is employed in the act of escaping, and
c whether the readers are invited to place their perspective inside or outside the depicted house.

| *After a rock struck her home in the Shifa neighbourhood, Maysa Muhammed, 47, escaped through the rubble.* | فرت ميساء محمد (47) من تحت الأنقاض بعد سقوط صاروخ على منزلها في حي الشفاء. |

Exercise 3: Read the following two *BBC* news items on the same topic (23 October 2017) to identify whether the events are viewed in both texts prospectively or retrospectively.

> *One of Russia's top radio presenters has had surgery after being stabbed in the neck by a man who broke into her newsroom at broadcaster Ekho Moskvy.*
>
> خضعت الإذاعية الروسية تاتيانا فلغينغايور لجراحة بعد أن طعنها في الرقبة شخص اقتحم غرفة الأخبار في مقر إذاعة إيكو موسكوفي.

Exercise 4: Read the following text extracted from a short story titled الشباك والساحة *The Window and the Courtyard* by Maḥmūd 'Abdulwahhāb (translated by and cited in Sadkhan and Pragnell 2012: 18–19) to identify in both texts:

a whether the readers are invited to place their perspective point inside or outside the classrooms,
b whether the readers adopt a distal, medial or proximal perspective, and
c whether the perspective point is in motion (sequential) or not (synoptic).

> *Two teachers passed us on their way to the classrooms; one of them shakes her head, the other listens. There is a heavy silence in the classroom. Our teacher came in, half her face covered by spectacles.*
>
> مرّت علينا معلمتان في طريقهما إلى الصفوف، تنود إحداهما برأسها والثانية تنصت. صمت ثقيل داخل الصف. دخلت معلمتنا تملأ نصف وجهها نظارة طبية ...

Further reading

Coulson, S. (2000). *Semantic Leaps: Frame-Shifting and Conceptual Blending in Meaning Construction*. Cambridge: Cambridge University Press.
Evans, V. (2007). *A Glossary of Cognitive Linguistics*. Edinburgh: Edinburgh University Press.
Evans, V. and Green, M. (2006). *Cognitive Linguistics: An Introduction*. Edinburgh: Edinburgh University Press.
Kress, G. and Hodge, R. (1979). *Language as Ideology*. London: Routledge and Kegan Paul.
Langacker, R. ([1991] 2002). *Concept, Image, Symbol: The Cognitive Basis of Grammar* (2nd edn). Berlin: Mouton de Gruyter.
Langacker, R. (2008). *Cognitive Grammar: A Basic Introduction*. Oxford: Oxford University Press.
Lee, D. (2001). *Cognitive Linguistics: An Introduction*. Oxford: Oxford University Press.
Leech, G. and Svartvik, J. (2002). *A Communicative Grammar of English*. London: Longman.
Talmy, L. (1985). "Force Dynamics in Language and Thought". In W. Eilfort, P. Kroeber and K. Peterson (eds.), *Papers from the Parasession on Causatives and Agentivity*, pp. 293–337. Chicago: Chicago Linguistics Society.
_____. (1988). "Force Dynamics in Language and Cognition", *Cognitive Science*, Vol. 12, pp. 49–100.
_____. (2000). *Toward a Cognitive Semantics: Vol. 1: Concept Structuring Systems*. Cambridge: MIT Press.
Taylor, J. (2002). *Cognitive Grammar*. Oxford: Oxford University Press.
Ungerer, H. and Friedrich, S. (1996). *An Introduction to Cognitive Linguistics*. London: Longman.

References

Almanna, A. and Al-Rubai'i, A. (2009; bilingual edn). *Modern Iraqi Short Stories: A Bilingual Reader*. London: Sayyab Books Ltd.
Almanna, A. and Hall, M. (2015; bilingual edn). *Moroccan Short Stories: A Bilingual Reader*. München: Lincom Europa Academic Publishers.
Coulson, S. (2000). *Semantic Leaps: Frame-Shifting and Conceptual Blending in Meaning Construction*. Cambridge: Cambridge University Press.
Croft, W. and Cruse, D. A. (2004). *Cognitive Linguistics*. Cambridge: Cambridge University Press.
de Saussure, F. (1916). *Cours de Linguistique Générale*. Paris: Editions Payot (translated in 1983 by R. Harris as *Course in General Linguistics*. London: Duckworth).
Evans, V. (2007). *A Glossary of Cognitive Linguistics*. Edinburgh: Edinburgh University Press.
Evans, V. and Green, M. (2006). *Cognitive Linguistics: An Introduction*. Edinburgh: Edinburgh University Press.
Hart, C. (2014). "Construal Operations in Online Press Reports of Political Protests". In C. Hart and P. Cap (eds.), *Contemporary Critical Discourse Studies*, pp. 167–188. London: Bloomsbury.
Husni, R. and Newman, D. (2008; bilingual edn). *Modern Arabic Short Stories: A Binigual Reader*. London: Saqi Books.
Kress, G. and Hodge, R. (1979). *Language as Ideology*. London: Routledge and Kegan Paul.
Langacker, R. ([1991] 2002). *Concept, Image, Symbol: The Cognitive Basis of Grammar* (2nd edn). Berlin: Mouton de Gruyter.
———. (2008). *Cognitive Grammar: A Basic Introduction*. Oxford: Oxford University Press.
Lee, D. (2001). *Cognitive Linguistics: An Introduction*. Oxford: Oxford University Press.
Leech, G. and Svartvik, J. (2002). *A Communicative Grammar of English*. London: Longman.
Pragnell, F. (2017; bilingual edn). الفراشة والزهرة '*The Butterfly and the Blossom*'. München: Lincom Europa Academic Publishers.
Pragnell, F. and Sadkhan, R. (2011). *Ten Stories from Iraq: A Bilingual Reader*. London: Sayyab Books Ltd.
Sadkhan, R. and Pragnell, F. (2012). رائحة الشتاء *The Scent of Winter: A Bilingual Reader*. London: Sayyab Books Ltd.
Talmy, L. (1985). "Force Dynamics in Language and Thought". In W. Eilfort, P. Kroeber and K. Peterson (eds.), *Papers from the Parasession on Causatives and Agentivity*, pp. 293–337. Chicago: Chicago Linguistics Society.
———. (1988). "Force Dynamics in Language and Cognition", *Cognitive Science*, Vol. 12, pp. 49–100.
———. (2000). *Toward a Cognitive Semantics: Vol. 1: Concept Structuring Systems*. Cambridge: MIT Press.
Taylor, J. (2002). *Cognitive Grammar*. Oxford: Oxford University Press.
Ungerer, H. and Friedrich, S. (1996). *An Introduction to Cognitive Linguistics*. London: Longman.
Zagood, M. and Pragnell, F. (2017; bilingual edn). أموت كلَّ يوم *I Die Every Day*. München: Lincom Europa Academic Publishers.

INDEX

'Abbas, Lu'aī Hamza 108, 112, 119
'Abdulwahhāb, Maḥmūd 23, 64, 74, 94, 100, 114, 125, 133, 135, 137, 139
'Abūd, Salām 117, 131
Accompaniment 86, 102
action schema 77, 91, 99–100, 124
actionalizing operations 116, 125, 138
active voice 127
Actor 9, 60–62, 74, 76–78, 84, 87–90, 94–98, 103, 117–119, 124, 126–127, 130, 132
adjective 68, 93, 107, 108, 116
adjunct 89–90
adverb 68, 71, 76, 95, 98, 108, 115
advertisement 3, 15–17, 20–22, 26–28, 35–37, 43–47, 50–54, 67, 77
Affected Participant 9, 61–62, 77, 83, 118–119, 132; Patient 83–85, 102, 127; Stimulus 84, 102
Affecting Participant 84, 102; see also stimulus
Agent 76–77, 83–84, 87, 92, 95, 99–100, 102, 118–119, 126–127, 132
agonist 128–129, 138
Al-'Uthmān, Laylā 63, 101
Al-Faqīh, Ibrāhīm 73, 123
Ali, Mary 69, 89
Al-Ja'kī, 'Alī Muḥammad 25, 28, 120, 128
allusion 48
Al-Ṣā'īgh, 'Adnān 73, 80, 104
Al-Ṣāni', Rajā' 75, 79
Al-Zafzāf, Muḥammad 24, 130
antagonist 128–129, 138

Arabic 3–4, 26, 29, 35, 37, 39–47, 54–56, 61–62, 67, 76–78, 89, 92, 96, 100, 102, 108, 111, 113, 119, 127, 129–130, 136–138
Arabic vernaculars 33
argument 4–5, 82–86, 88–92, 96, 98, 102–104, 116–119; see also noun phrase
as-Samhān, Latīf 49, 55
Associate (Predicate) 86, 102
atelicity 96, 117, 132; see also telicity
attention 5, 10, 27, 36, 41, 43, 55, 61, 67, 73, 82, 89–90, 98–99, 104, 122, 124–125, 127, 136, 138; backgrounded in 24, 61, 97, 100, 109, 122–126; foregrounded in 100, 122, 124, 126; see also backgrounding; distribution of attention; foregrounding; scope of attention; windowing of attention
attentional system 4, 106, 122
Attribute 68–69
axiality 2, 4, 106, 116, 119, 122

backgrounding 2, 24, 122
back-translation 7, 39–40
Baghdad 73–74
Bakr, Salwa 91, 108, 116, 124
BBC 28–29, 61, 76–77, 80, 92, 113–114, 120, 126–131, 138
Behaver 67–68, 74, 78, 98, 117
behavioural process (process of behaving) 4, 42, 59–60, 66–68, 74, 77–78, 98, 101, 117, 132
Benefactor (benefactive) 85, 102

Index

Bought, sth 88–90
boundedness, state of 2, 4, 106, 109–114, 119–120, 122, 126; *see also* bounding; debounding; excerpting; unboundedness; unbounding
bounding 119
Britain 51
Buyer 88, 90
Būzafūr, 'Ahmad 18, 110, 118

Carrier 68–69, 78
causality 128–129, 131; *see also* causation; extent of causation
causation 23, 85; *see also* causality; extent of causation
Causer 85, 102
China 39, 42
Choukri, M. 47
circumstances 4, 22, 59, 64, 67, 71–79, 82, 96, 115, 119, 130, 132
Client 60–62
closed path 123–124, 138
codes 14–16, 18, 50
cognitive operation 90, 107–108, 110–111, 114, 116, 119, 125, 134–136; synopticizing 135–136; unbounding 90, 107–108, 119
colour symbolism 39–43
combination, principle of 27; *see also* syntagms
commutation test 26–28
conceptual process 78
conceptualization processes; *see* imaging systems
configurational system 4–5, 106–120, 122; *see also* axiality; boundedness, state of; degree of extension; dividedness, state of; disposition of a quantity; pattern of distribution; plexity; scene partitioning/portioning
connotation 20–22, 33–34, 45, 53–54; *see also* iconic function; indexical function; symbolic function
construal operations; *see* imaging systems
content 42, 64–65, 94–95; *see also* Verbiage
Crawford, Cindy 46–47
cultural conventions 15, 17

debounding 110, 119
Decided, sth 88–89
Decider 88–89
degree of extension 2, 4, 106, 114, 119
denotation 33, 53–54
de-verbalization 6–7, 11

diagnostic components 20, 28
direction 2–3, 6, 35, 38, 55, 100–101, 132, 136–138; prospective 136–137; retrospective 136–137
disposition of a quantity 113–114; domain 106, 113, 125; *see also* boundedness, state of; dividedness, state of; plexity
distal perspective 10, 25, 68, 113–114, 134–136, 138
distance 2, 5, 10–11, 41, 52, 63, 71, 127, 132, 133–136; *see also* zooming
distribution of attention 5, 122–127, 138
dividedness, state of 2, 4, 106, 112–113, 119, 122

Egypt 41, 76–77, 99
energy transfer 2, 5, 77, 91, 98–102; and mental contact 98, 101–102; *see also* flow of energy
English 3, 4, 8, 10–11, 16, 36, 39–40, 44–47, 50, 52, 54, 56, 61–62, 68, 76–79, 86, 92, 102, 104, 113, 120, 127, 130, 138
Eubank, Chris 50–52
excerpting 110–111, 119
existential 36, 78
existential process (process of existing) 4, 59–60, 70–71, 77–78, 98–99
Experiencer 83–84, 91, 96, 101–103
extent of causation 2, 5, 24–25, 27–28, 73–74, 77, 89, 109, 122–124, 138; *see also* causality; causation.
external reality 32–33

figure-ground organization 122, 138
flow of energy 82, 98–101; bidirectional 99–100; unidirectional 77, 91, 99–100, 124; *see also* energy transfer
force dynamics 2, 36, 73, 89, 122, 128–132, 138
force-dynamic patterns 5, 128–131, 138
force-dynamic pressure 129–130
force-dynamic system 4, 106, 122
force-dynamic value 36, 89, 138
foregrounding 2, 24, 122
functional grammar 1–2; *see also* Halliday's systemic functional grammar

gapping 24, 61, 87, 124–125, 127
Given, sth 86
Giver 86
Goal 60–62, 74–77, 85–86, 88–89, 95, 97, 102–103, 122, 127, 132
Granted, sth 89
Grantee 89

Index

Granter 89
Guthrie, Alice 70, 104

Hall, Bridget 44, 77
Halliday, M. A. K. 59, 62, 71, 100
Halliday's systemic functional grammar 4–5, 59
Hawthorne, Nathaniel 19, 29, 65, 79

iconic function 2, 4, 32, 34–35, 39, 42, 54
iconicity 34, 44–45
imaging systems 4, 106, 122, 126, 128; *see also* attentional system; configurational system; force-dynamic system; perspectival system
indeterminacy theory 8, 11
index 36–37; definition 36
indexical function 2, 4, 32, 34, 36–39, 54
Instrument 11, 83–84, 92–93, 102–103, 118
Integrant 86, 118
interpretant 32–33, 41, 48, 54
interpretive approach 3, 6–7, 11; *see also* de-verbalization; re-expression (reformulation); understanding; verification
interpretive frame 77
interpretive semiotics 2, 32, 54
intertextual links 51–54
intertextual reference 50–52, 54
intertextual space 48
intertextuality 2, 32, 47–54; definition 47
intertexual relation/relationship 4, 32, 41, 47–49, 51, 55
Iraq 37, 62, 96
Iraqi dialect 17, 33
IS *see* ISIS
ISIS/Islamic State 62, 70, 104, 131
Islam 43, 70, 89

Kristeva, Julia 47, 50
Küng, Hans 65, 99

lexemes 20; diagnostic 19–20; supplementary 20
lexical item 19, 23, 29, 33, 41, 62, 90, 95–96, 110, 112, 117, 125
linguistics 1; cognitive 1–2, 106
location (locative) 2, 5, 50, 71, 83, 85, 95–98, 102–103, 117–118, 127, 132–133; *see also* perspective point

magnification 114, 119
Mahfouz, N. 40–41, 48, 55, 101, 103, 115, 134

material process (process of doing) 4, 38, 42, 59–62, 66–67, 74–79, 83, 86, 94–97, 108–109, 117–119, 126–127, 132
meaning 7–8, 14–17, 20–22, 26–28, 33, 37–38, 43, 45, 47, 53–54, 59, 67, 92–93, 99; relations 38; *see also* connotation; denotation
medial perspective 134, 138
mental contact 98, 101–102
mental image 2–5, 7–11, 17–19, 23–24, 27, 41, 59–61, 67, 73, 75–77, 79, 82, 89–91, 93, 95–96, 98–99, 101–102, 108, 110–111, 113, 123, 126–127
mental process (process of sensing) 4, 59–60, 62–64, 72, 78, 83, 88, 91, 191, 130; cognition 62–63; desideration 62–63; emotion 34, 62, 83–84, 102; perception 47, 59, 62–63, 128
metonymy 21, 28
mode 2, 132, 135–136; sequential 135, 138–139; synoptic 135–136, 138–139
Muhammad, Prophet 41
multiplexity 67, 74, 90, 101, 106–108, 110, 115, 119, 125; iterated 125

narrative 2, 77, 98, 126
Nāṣir, 'Abdulsattār 91, 107
Nescafé 21, 50–54
noun phrase 4, 9, 11, 63, 69, 82, 90, 91–93; *see also* argument

Obama, Barack 29
Oman 37, 96
Omega watches 46–47
open path 61, 77, 87–88, 122–125, 127, 138
Opened, sth 117

pace of events 5, 23–24, 27–28, 73–74, 98
paradigm 18–22, 26–28; *see also* paradigmatic axis
paradigmatic axis 2–5, 14, 18–29
paradigmatic relationships 21–22
Paris School 6
passive voice 62, 127
Patek Philippe watch Twenty~4 44–46, 77–78
paths 5, 61, 85, 122–124; closed 123–124, 138; motion 109; open 61, 77, 87–88, 122–125, 127, 138; types of 87
pattern of distribution 2, 4, 106, 115–116, 119, 122
Peirce, C. S. 32–35, 38, 48
Peirce's interpretive semiotics 32–47; *see also* iconic function; indexical function; symbolic function

Peircean model 16
personation type 116–119; dyadic 116–117; monadic 116–119
perspectival system 2, 4, 25, 106, 122, 136, 138; schematic categories of 2, 132, 135–136; *see also* direction; distance; location; mode
perspective 5, 122; deployment of 5, 132–137; distal 10, 25, 68, 113–114, 134–136, 138; medial 134, 138; proximal 11, 114, 133–135, 138–139; *see also* direction; distance; location; mode; perspective point
perspective point 124, 132–133, 135–137, 139; exterior 132; interior 132
photographers 3
picture-taking 3–4, 6
plexity 2, 4, 98, 106–109, 113, 119, 125; definition 106; *see also* multiplexity; uniplexity
Positioner 86, 95, 102
possessive attributive process 69, 77–78
Possessor 62, 69, 86, 102–103
Predicate (Associate) 86, 102
prepositional phrase 9, 69, 71, 93, 95
profile selection 2, 122
proximal perspective11, 114, 133–135, 138–139
Puigdemont, Carles 127–128, 130

Quine, Willard Van Orman 8
Quranic verses 48–49

Received, sth 87
Receiver 64–66, 86–87, 117, 124
Recipient 60–61, 75, 77, 85, 87–89, 102–103, 117, 124
reduction 114, 119
re-expressing 6–7, 11
re-expression (reformulation) 7
reification 116, 125, 138
relational process (process of being/having) 4, 59–62, 68–70, 75–79, 93–95, 117, 127; attributive 68–69, 77–78; identifying 68
relationships: iconic 34, 38, 44–45; indexical 36–37, 39, 44, 47; symbolic 35, 39, 43–44; *see also* intertextual relations/relationships; paradigmatic relationships; syntagmatic relationships
representamen 32
Resultant (effect) 85, 102
retrospective direction 136–138
Reuters 62

Saudi Arabia 77
Saussure, Ferdinand de 16–18, 32
Saussurean model 16
Sayer 19, 42, 64–66, 72, 76, 79, 94–95, 116, 126
scene partitioning/portioning 2, 4, 106, 116–120, 122
schematic category 113, 132–133, 135–136; *see also* direction; distance; location; mode; perspective
schematic systems *see* imaging systems
scope of attention 2, 23–24, 97, 122–123, 135; global 135; local 135
scope of intention 2, 5, 23–25, 27–28, 73–74, 77, 89, 109, 122–124, 138
scope of prediction 24, 124
selection, principle of (paradigms) 27
Seller 88–89
semantic cases 82, 102; *see also* semantic roles
semantic domain 125
semantic roles 2, 4–5, 11, 61, 82–104, 117–119, 124, 126–127, 132; action tier of 88; and grammatical relations 90–98; thematic tier of 88; types of 82; verb-specific 86–90; *see also* Accompaniment; Actor; Affected Participant; Agent; Attribute; Behaver; Causer; Carrier; Client; Experiencer; Giver; Goal; Integrant; Instrument; Positioner; Possessor; Predicate; Receiver; Recipient; Sayer; semantic cases; Sender; Senser; Source; Stimulus; Theme; thematic roles; theta roles
semantics 1–2
semiotics 1–2, 14–28, 32, 35, 38; definition 14; pragmatic 15; semantic 15; social 38; structural 2, 28; syntactic 15; *see also* interpretive semiotics
Sender 87, 117, 124
sense theory 11; *see also* interpretive approach
Senser 62–64, 67, 72, 79, 102, 130
Sent, sth 87, 117
sign 2–5, 14–28, 32, 34–35, 38–39, 41–42, 46–51; definition 14; iconic 34; indexical 34; symbolic 34; functions of 32; *see also* commutation test; paradigm; Peirce's interpretive semiotics; signified; signifier; syntagm
signified 2–3, 16–18, 28, 32, 34–36, 38, 41
signifier 2–3, 15–18, 20–22, 26, 28, 32, 38, 41
signifying system 14, 49–50
slot-and-filler principle 22–23, 28

Sold, sth 88–89
Source 73, 85–86, 88–89, 97, 102–103, 123, 127
Spain 127–129
Standard Arabic 33
state of being 4–5, 59–60, 113, 127, 129
state of existing 4–5, 59–60
state of mind 4–5, 59–60, 62
Stimulus 84, 91, 101–103; *see also* Affecting Participant
strength of attention 122
structural semiotics 2, 28
Sudan 37
supplementary components 20, 28
symbolic function 2, 4, 32, 34, 39–47, 54
symbols 14, 34, 39, 43–44, 46, 49; local 43–44; universal 43–44
synecdoche 21, 28
syntactic structure 9, 11, 89
syntagm 18–25, 27–28; *see also* syntagmatic axis
syntagmatic axis 2–5, 14, 18–29, 32
syntagmatic relationships 20–21; sequential 20; spatial 20, 71, 88, 96; temporal 20, 71
Syria 99, 131
system of voice 100; effective 100; middle 100

Talmy, Leonard 4, 106, 113, 115, 125, 135–136
Tāmir, Zakariyyā 67, 110, 133
telicity 96–97; *see also* atelicity
thematic roles 82, 103; *see also* semantic roles
Theme 11, 83–84, 87–90, 95–97, 102–103, 117–118
theory of sense 6; *see also* interpretive approach
theta roles 82, 102; *see also* semantic roles
time gap 75, 132; *see also* time lapse; time interval
time interval 64, 94, 95; *see also* time gap; time lapse

time lapse 5, 24, 61, 74–75, 80, 98; *see also* time gap; time interval
transitivity 16, 59–60, 79; definition 59; *see also* behavioural processes; existential processes; material processes; mental processes; relational processes; transitivity processes; verbal processes
transitivity processes 4–5, 19, 59, 126
transitivity system 2, 59–79, 82; *see also* circumstances; transitivity
translation 1–10, 14–15, 19, 25, 29, 32, 34, 42, 47–48, 55, 59–60, 75, 80, 89, 91–92, 95–96, 100, 102–104, 106, 108, 111, 113, 119–120, 135–138; accuracy 4–5, 19, 23, 28, 32, 59, 73; Arabic 46–47; 'intralingual' 34; process 7, 34; *see also* back-translation
Tunisia 48, 99
Turkey 99

UK, the 17, 37, 43, 51–52, 71, 86
unboundedness 109–111, 119
unbounding 90, 107–108, 119
understanding 6–7, 11
UNHCR 100, 111, 119, 136, 138
uniplexity 67, 101, 106–108, 113, 119

van Outen, Denise 51–52
verbal process (process of saying) 4, 19, 42, 59–60, 64–66, 72, 76, 79, 94, 95, 116, 126
Verbiage 19, 42, 64–66, 72, 76, 79, 94–95, 116, 126; of the process 19, 42, 65–66, 72, 94–95, 116, 126; *see also* content
verification 7, 11
visual grammar 1–2

windowing of attention 2, 5, 27–28, 98, 122–124, 138
Wright, Ian 51–52

Yemen 33, 37, 115, 126
Yusuf, Prophet 49–50

zooming 134, 138